# Gilding Crafts

# Gilding Crafts

Glorious effects with gold and
silver in over 40 step-by-step
ideas and projects

*Liz Wagstaff*

aqua marine

This edition is published by Aquamarine, an imprint of Anness Publishing Ltd, Blaby Road, Wigston, Leicestershire LE18 4SE; info@anness.com

www.aquamarinebooks.com; www.annesspublishing.com

If you like the images in this book and would like to investigate using them for publishing, promotions or advertising, please visit our website www.practicalpictures.com for more information.

Publisher: JOANNA LORENZ
Senior Editor: LINDSAY PORTER
Designer: LISA TAI
Photographer and Stylist: DEBBIE PATTERSON
Step Photographer: LUCY TIZARD
Original pieces supplied by: LILLIE CURTISS (page 12 bottom left and top, page 18 bottom right) LYNETTE SMART (page 12 bottom right), CATHERINE PURVES (page 13 top) and MARK THURGOOD (page 13 right).

© Anness Publishing Ltd 2013

A CIP catalogue record for this book is available from the British Library.

PUBLISHER'S NOTE
Although the advice and information in this book are believed to be accurate and true at the time of going to press, neither the authors nor the publisher can accept any legal responsibility or liability for any errors or omissions that may have been made nor for any inaccuracies nor for any loss, harm or injury that comes about from following instructions or advice in this book.

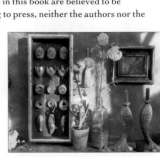

# CONTENTS

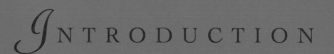

# INTRODUCTION

*Gilding is an ancient technique with an illustrious pedigree. Despite the advent of alternative metallic finishes, the traditional method is still used by many designers and craftspeople today.*

# THE GILDER'S ART

Gilding with real gold leaf has been a popular form of decoration for many centuries. It was first used by the ancient Egyptians and many examples of their beautiful work can be seen in museums worldwide. Because of the high cost of gold, less expensive metals have been developed in leaf form as substitutes for gilding.

Traditional techniques take time and care to master but are well worth the patience and dexterity required to produce items of beauty. The substitute metals and newer techniques, however, can be just as effective and, when applied well, give similarly attractive results.

Even with the steady rise in the cost of gold and the introduction of substitute leaf and powders, the popularity of real gold leaf has not waned. The main reason appears to be that much of the new leaf looks good immediately after application, but it can quickly lose its brilliance on exposure to the air, while real gold leaf does not tarnish and can be restored to its original state when it becomes dirty by washing.

Many forms of real gold leaf come in combination with substitute leaf, and bronze powders are also available. They all come in a wide range of colours and tones, so that many different finishes can be achieved. With the advances in technology, many wild and wonderful colours are readily available in craft shops, enabling the gilder to produce fantasy finishes quite easily.

Gold is very malleable and can be beaten into extremely thin sheets to make metallic leaf. Other metals are not so easily influenced and give thicker sheets that can be cut with scissors. Real gold leaf is so fine that it needs to be handled with great care and it requires special tools. These have not changed for centuries, giving the art of gilding a charming, timeless quality.

The use of substitute leaf and powders makes the art more accessible and it can be applied to transform all manner of objects. New paints and primers have widened the scope for the surfaces that can be gilded, as previously unsuitable objects can now be prepared to take the leaf.

New developments in leaf and powders, gold pastes and sprays have developed rapidly over the last few years. By applying some of the finishing techniques explained in this book, these less traditionally gilded items will sit quite happily among those decorated by more advanced processes. Experiment with different techniques on dried flowers and foliage, vases and candle holders to create a shimmering array in your home.

*Right: Humble objects are transformed into objects of beauty with gilding.*

# $\mathcal{T}$HE HISTORY OF GILDING

The ancient Egyptians were the first to begin experimenting with gold embellishment. Examples of gilding have been found in the tombs of the pharaohs, the oldest dating back over 3000 years. Probably the most famous is the gilded mask of Tutankhamen.

Until the eighteenth century and the discovery of platinum, gold was the most precious of metals. The art of gilding was developed to apply layers of precious metals on to cheaper materials, such as wood or plaster.

The Italians' use of gold leaf in the Middle Ages was one of the most beautiful and the use of a deep red gesso base gave their gilding a richness of colour seldom achieved elsewhere. Fine examples of this form of gilding

*Above: This nineteenth century French gilded cockerel is a fine example of the ornate effects possible with gilding.*

can be seen on the frames of medieval Italian religious paintings as well as on the panels of triptychs used as altar pieces.

It was also the Italians in the late sixteenth century who produced a gold effect by applying a varnish tinted with yellow over silver or white metal leaf. This technique is still used in the work of fairground decorators, although today the metal used is usually aluminium.

During the nineteenth century, a leaf made from an alloy of zinc and copper called Dutch metal was developed as a substitute for gold. It is still used today when a gold effect is required, at a fraction of the cost. It is not effective on items that will be exposed to extreme weathering, as it tends to deteriorate.

*Above: Gilded chimney piece in the Long Gallery, Lancaster House, London, built in the early nineteenth century.*

*Right: The main hall of Igumnov Mansion, Moscow, built in the late nineteenth century.*

In Britain, gilding has been used as a form of decoration since the Stuart period. It appears in its most decorative form in baroque and rococo interiors and was at its most splendid in the homes of continental Europeans. English taste was more modest; gilt furniture and decoration was considered ostentatious until the end of the seventeenth century.

At the beginning of the eighteenth century, gilding played an important part in the

*Above: The ballroom of Kharitonenko Mansion, Moscow. Gold has been used to embellish all architectural details.*

decoration of classical interiors. Columns, mouldings and other architectural details were emphasized by gilding in different tones, depending on the colour of bole or gesso underneath.

Gilding was used by eminent English architects to decorate the ballrooms and state apartments of great houses. Chinoiserie, with its

strong oriental influence, was a popular form of decoration in eighteenth-century Europe and gilding was used in combination with lacquer techniques to produce decorative items.

Throughout the nineteenth and twentieth centuries, gilding evolved to adapt to the different styles in interior decoration. The sumptuous finish of gilding can still be used to glittering effect in our modern age, in contemporary or traditional interiors.

11

# CONTEMPORARY GILDING

Gilding is easily adapted to suit modern interiors and the ever-changing trends in design. The choice of surface and different methods of application can create an amazing variety of finishes, especially when gilding is used on surprising objects. Famous designers such as Christian Lacroix and Donna Karan enjoy playing with gilding in their homes and Christian Lacroix's extravagant jewellery and glitzy clothes reflect his love of gold.

Gilding is as fashionable today as it has ever been and it always adds a touch of glamour and style to a room. Mix gilding with contemporary furniture and

*Above: The clean simple lines of this glass topped gilded table are the perfect foil for the gilded finish.*

objets d'art to produce a stunning new look. Many decorators and designers promote the craft of gilding in their creations, often choosing the most unusual objects to decorate in this way. Even stark modern interiors can be enhanced by the use of gilding. Designers have experimented with gilding on natural objects such as driftwood, shells and stones to fit in with a minimalist style.

At the other extreme, historical influences are still very much in evidence in contemporary gilding and much of the work of modern designers has its roots in classical and gothic styles as featured in many of today's interior decoration magazines. The recent trend towards fun and kitsch furniture and interiors has also enhanced the popularity of gilding, while the gothic revival

has inspired many people to scour markets and junk shops for items in an ecclesiastical style to gild and adorn their homes.

The new colours available in substitute metals and metallic powders have provided great scope for experimentation. Copper and aluminium leaf can be applied to modern furniture for a stylish effect. Gilded furniture can also be mixed with modern upholstery and materials with stunning results. When combined with paint effects, simple aluminium leaf can be transformed to give the appearance of iron or lead. Rust, verdigris and other patination finishes are all easy to achieve,

*Above: These striking contemporary gilded chairs are based on the alchemical symbols for gold.*

*Above: The fibreboard frame of this medieval-style mirror is decorated with metal leaf and aged with acrylic paint.*

*Above: These steel lights, decorated with male and female figures, are gilded in gold and aluminium Dutch metal leaf.*

and they complement gilding in the modern home. New designers apply gilding to a wide variety of surfaces including ceramics and papier mâché. It is not unusual to see a whole door or window frame gilded, as cheaper metals make decorating large areas with gilding a viable undertaking, and it is very difficult to tell the difference between these cheaper finishes and the more costly ones.

The craft of gilding has opened up a whole new world of ideas for interior designers. It is a pleasing thought that this age-old art, first developed by the Egyptians, has retained its allure and is certain to continue to capture the artistic imagination in the future.

*Right: These wooden star clocks are decorated in gold and silver leaf, and aged with acrylic colour. The crown clock is made from chemically patinated copper and broken Dutch metal leaf.*

# BASIC TECHNIQUES

*Once you have decided that you would like to gild an object, you need to choose the look you would like to achieve. Pure gold leaf will stand the test of time, but powders and pastes add instant dazzle.*

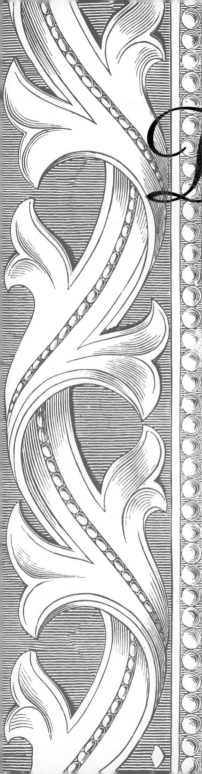

# GILDING EFFECTS

The purity of gold leaf is measured in carats. The number of carats signifies the number of parts of pure gold in the metal, which is most commonly thought of as containing 24 parts. Pure gold contains 24 parts gold out of 24 and so is 24-carat gold. As other metals are added, the purity decreases, giving different colours of gold such as white, pale lemon and mid-green. Gold is also available in different weights and thicknesses. Apart from the differences in weight and colour, gold leaf is supplied in two forms called loose and transfer. Loose leaf comes in sheets between rouged paper. The pack or book of loose leaf needs to be carefully handled so that the leaves do not slide out. In the case of transfer leaf, a rectangle of tissue larger than the leaf is placed in each opening of the book and the book is then compressed so that the gold adheres to the tissue. Transfer leaf is the leaf most commonly used by amateur gilders. It was always considered a safer option by craftspeople working out of doors, as there was less chance of the precious metal disappearing in a gust of wind.

Transfer leaf is the only leaf suitable for oil gilding but it is not available in such a wide range of weights and colours as loose leaf. Although loose leaf requires a larger initial outlay for equipment, it can be used on surfaces where it is difficult to apply transfer leaf. If you are only planning to gild one or two small items, transfer leaf may well be the cheaper option, but if you start gilding on a regular basis, it is a good idea to master the skills of cutting and handling loose leaf.

The cost of gold leaf varies greatly and often depends on where you buy it, the weight, the retailer and the country of origin. Some ordinary art suppliers stock gold leaf but a wider selection will be available from gilding sundries suppliers or goldbeaters.

It does not always pay to use inferior gold. Experienced gilders can achieve pleasing results using a cheaper leaf but it is only due to their skill in handling the metal. Beginners should use loose double-weight gold, which will withstand rougher treatment.

Silver and other metal leaf comes in slightly larger sheets than gold. Like gold, it is sold in books of 25 leaves. Due to the properties of other metals, they cannot be beaten as thinly as gold and have to be sealed and varnished once they have been laid. Silver or copper leaf is often sealed with clear varnish to preserve its appearance. Silver leaf that is sealed with yellow varnish takes

*Above: Dutch metal transfer leaf is used to add embellishment to wax candles.*

on the appearance of gold. Silver leaf should be carefully wrapped when stored, to protect it from the air. The edges may need trimming to remove the dark lines that might be visible during laying.

From the Middle Ages to the eighteenth century, tin was a popular metal for its bright white, non-tarnishing finish. Today white gold, platinum, palladium and aluminium are more likely to be used instead. Platinum is very

expensive and is available only in small sheets, as is palladium. Aluminium is cheaper and is available in larger sheets. It has a slightly greyish colour. White gold can be beaten thinner than any of the other metals and gives the most brilliant surface.

Schlag leaf, more commonly known as Dutch metal, is quite a thick leaf made from a zinc and copper alloy. It is available in shades of copper, red and yellow.

This leaf tarnishes quite easily and should be well varnished if required for more than a temporary finish. As this leaf is cheap, it is quite often used for theatrical props and sets. It can be bought in packs of 25–500 leaves and there is usually no interleaving tissue, so it should be well wrapped when stored.

Gold can also be bought ground up and mixed with a small amount of gum arabic and formed into small tablets. This form of gold is expensive and mainly used for restoration purposes. Gold in powder form was once used for japan work but is not now readily available. It is possible to make your own but this is quite time-consuming and not really necessary due to the wide range of other materials on the market. Bronze powders, on the other hand, are easy to obtain and come in several varieties and colours. They tarnish quite quickly and must be varnished. There are tarnish-resistant makes but these are expensive. The colours range from pale gold to copper and antique bronze. Ordinary powdered bronzes usually have larger flakes, while lining bronzes are finer and burnishing bronzes are finer still.

If you want to produce a look similar to real gold leaf but in a third of the time and with little preparation, you could choose Dutch metal or another substitute metal. The beauty of the gold colour then needs to be enhanced using shellac varnish but the results can be stunning. It is also possible to produce deceptively authentic-looking pieces using paint techniques and distressing.

If you choose real gold leaf, the proper tools and materials are essential – you cannot cut on the cost if you wish to achieve a perfect look. Using the incorrect tools and materials may not give you the results you had hoped for, and could be a very expensive mistake. Any leaf will need fixing. This should be taken into consideration when you are choosing to gild an object that will either be kept outside or be exposed to wear and tear.

The size of the area to be gilded should also be taken into consideration when choosing materials. If you wish to cover a large object, the expense of using real gold leaf could be prohibitive, while a substitute leaf will give an equally pleasing result.

Pastes and powders are both readily available in a wide variety of colours and tones of gold, copper, bronze and silver. Liquid leaf is another good alternative when time and cost are important issues. Whichever material you decide to use, buy the best you can afford from a reputable supplier who can advise you on materials.

Gold pastes, paints and sprays are also widely available. They don't produce quite the same effect as gilding and lose their lustre, but are worth considering as a cheap alternative to gilding.

Whichever technique you choose, the surface to be gilded needs to be properly prepared. For the best results, follow the preparation instructions in the techniques section for your chosen effect.

*Above: This gilded mirror with candle sconces is given an aged effect to complement the gothic design.*

# MATERIALS

**Acrylic paints:** Like oil paints, the more expensive the paint, the more intense and fast the colours. Dilute acrylic paints with water and mix them with emulsion (latex paint) for different effects.

**Bronze, aluminium and silver powders:** These fine particles of metal can be mixed with varnish or blown or brushed on. They can be mixed with an ormoline medium for fabric painting.

**Ceramic tile adhesive:** Used for fixing tiles, mosaic pieces and other small objects to surfaces, this adhesive is available in a waterproof form if required.

**Edible leaf or warq:** This real gold or silver leaf is made by hammering and flattening small balls of gold or silver into very thin sheets and is used to decorate Indian food for ceremonies.

**Eggshell paint:** An oil-based paint that needs an oil-based undercoat. It gives a surface suitable for oil-based glazes and oil paints. Clean and dilute with white spirit (paint thinner).

**Filler:** This comes in various grades and is used to fill cracks or holes in wood and plaster. Filler dries to a hard, resilient surface, but is not as smooth as putty.

**French enamel varnish:** This is available in many different tones and colours, the most common of which is amber. It can be used to seal and protect gilded items and to change or enhance the colour and help create an aged effect.

**Gesso:** This fine chalk powder is the key ingredient of gesso solution. White or coloured ready-made acrylic gessos are also now available.

**Gilding water:** Made from water, methylated spirit (methyl alcohol) and rabbit skin size, this liquid is used in water gilding.

**Gold leaf:** This is available as loose or transfer leaf, in books of 25 leaves. Gold leaf is available in many weights and thicknesses and is classed in carats.

**Gold and silver paints:** These are made in the same way as liquid leaf but from cheaper materials. They are useful for stencilling and for decorative painting.

**Gold pastes:** These are available in many forms and in tones of gold, silver and aluminium. Often used in restoration work.

**Graphite powder:** When added to paints and varnishes this powder gives a deep grey to black metallic effect.

**Liquid leaf:** This mixture of metallic powder and deep red primer can be used to cover a wide variety of surfaces. It comes in many shades.

**Methylated spirit (methyl alcohol):** This is used to clean brushes after using polishes and some oil-based primers. It is also used to dilute gilding water and for distressing gilded surfaces.

**Oil-based size or japan gold size:** This size can be bought in various drying times. The longer the drying time, the shinier the gold will be when applied. This size is more resilient than water-based size.

**Oil paints:** The more expensive the oil paints are, the more intense and fast the colours. Dilute oil paints with varnish, white spirit (paint thinner) or linseed oil.

**Powder pigment:** Finely ground pure pigment is used to mix paints and tint water- or oil-based paints and varnishes.

**Rabbit skin size:** This comes in granule form and constitutes part of the mix for gesso and gilding water.

**Red clay:** This gives a smooth surface for water gilding and also comes in yellow, black and blue.

**Red oxide metal primer:** This primer (available in spray form and in different colours) is the ideal base coat for metal before applying paint or substitute leaf. It prevents rust and allows paint to take to the surface.

**Rottenstone:** This stone-coloured powder is used in the antiquing process and is usually applied to areas with a large amount of moulding and detail.

**Schlag or composition leaf (Dutch metal):** This looks like gold leaf but is cheaper. It is made from a copper and zinc alloy.

**Scumble glazes:** Available in water-based and oil-based mixes, these glazes produce a translucent effect and lengthen the working time of the water- and oil-based paints widely used for decorative paint effects.

**Shellac and polishes:** These come in many guises, such as button polish and transparent polish. They can be used to seal and protect gold but they will affect the colour.

**Silver, copper and aluminium leaf:** These leaves come in books of 25–500 loose or transfer leaves.

**Spray paints:** Oil- and water-based spray paints come in a vast range of colours.

**Talc:** Fine powdered talc is used in a pounce bag to cover a surface before sizing to make sure that the area is clean and that the leaf will only adhere to the sized areas.

**Undercoat:** Oil-based and quick-drying water-based undercoats are both available and provide a base coat for the appropriate top coat. The primer stabilizes the surface in preparation for paint.

**Varnishes:** Oil-based and water-based varnishes come in various finishes from matt to gloss.

**Water-based size:** A fast-drying synthetic size used for oil gilding and with bronze powders.

**Waxes:** Used as sealants or to protect gilded objects. Coloured waxes can change the tone of a gilded object.

**White spirit (paint thinner):** Used to dilute oil-based paints and varnishes.

*Right: Sizes, undercoats, gessos, and gold leaf and powders, all tools of a gilder.*

# EQUIPMENT

**Agate burnishers:** These are made from a small piece of agate mounted in brass on a wooden handle and are available in various sizes and shapes. They are rubbed over water-gilded surfaces to obtain a high and brilliant shine.

**Brushes:** Different brushes will be needed for different purposes:
*Badger brushes* are very expensive. A cheaper and environmentally friendly alternative is lily bristle. These brushes are used for softening glazes and varnishes. They should be cleaned and treated with care.
*Bristle brushes* are inexpensive, hard-wearing, can be used for applying a wide range of paints, glazes and varnishes, and are available in varying sizes.
*Gilder's tips* are wide, soft brushes used to pick up real gold leaf before applying it to a surface.
*Hog's-hair brushes* are available in various shapes and sizes with flat or round heads for mixing and applying clay colours.
*Decorator's brushes* can be used for applying paints, undercoats and varnishes.
*Sable brushes* are quite costly but are invaluable for detailed painting and decoration.
*Stencil brushes* are short-haired, coarse-bristled brushes used for stencil designs.

*Stippling brushes* are expensive brushes made of pure bristle used for taking dust off glazes.
*Sword liners* are designed for painting decorative lines on furniture and for producing veins on marbling.

**Cloths:** Cotton rags are the best type of cloths for use in gilding and producing other decorative finishes. Cotton dusters are ideal for burnishing delicate surfaces.

**Cotton wool balls:** Use these for pressing real gold leaf into place and for small cleaning up jobs.

**Double boiler or bain marie:** Used for melting beeswax pellets, ready-made gessos and sizes.

**Dust sheets and newspaper:** Use either to protect your room and work surface during gilding and painting projects.

**Flower mister:** Use this to spray water or methylated spirit (methyl alcohol) on to surfaces to disperse oil-based or water-based glazes.

**Gilder's knife:** This specialist knife is used to cut loose leaf.

**Gilder's pad:** This soft pad is surrounded by a screen of parchment or a similar paper screen to shield gold leaf from draughts.

**Gloves:** Heavy-duty household gloves are useful for stripping wood and for patination. Use disposable gloves for smaller decorative gilding jobs.

**Glues:** Epoxy resin glue, rubber-based glue and PVA glue are all useful in decorative work. It is worth having a collection of different types.

**Mask:** Wear a mask when working with bronze powders, sprays and some oil-based glazes. Masks are also useful when working in confined areas with any oil-based products.

**Masking tape:** Use a low-tack tape for masking off areas and securing stencils.

**Measuring tools, pens and pencils:** Necessary for stencilling and doing decorative painting.

**Mutton cloth:** Available in roll form, this cloth can be used for many decorative finishes and for cleaning up.

**Natural sponge:** Sea sponges are used to produce a variety of decorative finishes.

**Paint pots:** Paint pots are available in metal or plastic for mixing paints and glazes. Oil-based paints and glazes should not be stored in plastic.

**Sandpaper:** This abrasive paper comes in different grades for smoothing as well as producing an adhesive key for finishes. Wet-and-dry sandpaper is the best type for use on furniture and other items to be gilded.

**Scalpels and craft knives:** Collect various types of scalpel and craft knife for decorative work and for cutting stencils.

**Steel (wire) wool:** This abrasive mix of metal fibres comes in different grades for smoothing and providing a key for finishes. It is also used for distressing gilded surfaces with methylated spirit (methyl alcohol).

*Above: A selection of brushes, plus other gilding essentials such as a craft knife, and gloves for small decorating jobs.*

**Stencil cardboard:** Made from manilla coated in boiled oil, this specialist cardboard is used for making stencils.

# WATER GILDING

THE AGE-OLD TECHNIQUE OF WATER GILDING IS DIFFICULT TO MASTER, BUT THE RESULTS ARE TRULY MAGNIFICENT. THE SECRET TO SUCCESSFUL RESULTS LIES IN THE PREPARATION OF THE SURFACE PRIOR TO GILDING. BOTH GOLD AND SILVER CAN BE APPLIED USING THIS METHOD, FIXED WITH A SIMPLE GILDING WATER WHICH IS MADE BY ADDING A SMALL AMOUNT OF METHYLATED SPIRIT (METHYL ALCOHOL) TO WATER. THIS TECHNIQUE SHOULD BE CONFINED TO SMALL AREAS, AND IS NOT SUITABLE FOR LARGE PIECES. GESSO IS USED TO PREPARE THE SURFACE BEFORE APPLICATION – IT GIVES A TOUGH, RESISTANT, YET PERFECTLY SMOOTH SURFACE TO WORK ON. WOODEN FRAMES AND PLASTER DETAILS ARE IDEAL FIRST PROJECTS

1 Make sure that the surface you are gilding is clean and dry. Fill any cracks or holes with putty or filler and sand when dry. Melt rabbit skin size granules in a bain marie. This will take approximately 5–10 minutes. When the granules are completely dissolved, the size will be the consistency of runny caramel. Sift just enough gesso powder into the melted granules to colour the liquid. Heat over the bain marie until the liquid is translucent. Paint on to the surface so that it takes into the grain and leave the object to dry overnight.

2 Melt two parts rabbit skin size to one part water. Take off the heat and sift in enough gesso to come above the liquid. Put back on the heat and stir well with a brush to disperse all the lumps. While still warm, apply to the surface. Apply up to 12 coats. Each coat will take 10–15 minutes to dry. Try to complete this stage on the same day and leave the final coat to dry overnight. Alternatively, apply up to 12 coats of ready-made gesso in white or your chosen colour.

**3** To make the gilding water, half fill a jar with water. Slowly add methylated spirit (methyl alcohol) until the water is lightly coloured. Add 5ml/1 tsp of melted rabbit skin size. Stir until the solution is thoroughly mixed. Paint a small amount on to the area you wish to gild. It will enable the leaf to adhere to the surface.

**4** Gently place loose gold leaf on to the dampened surface and press down lightly with cotton (wool) balls. Continue painting on the gilding water and applying the gold leaf until the whole area is covered. Any small bare patches can be covered using a sable brush and small pieces of leaf. Leave to dry for 1 hour.

**5** When the surface is dry, burnish with an agate burnisher, going over the surface several times until a deep shine begins to appear. Do not press too hard as this will soften the gesso.

**6** To distress the surface to give an aged effect, gently rub the surface with wire (steel) wool. Do not rub too hard and take care only to distress the areas that would receive wear naturally.

**7** Seal the whole surface with clear wax. Leave to dry, and then polish with a soft cloth to improve the lustre.

# OIL GILDING

OIL GILDING CAN BE UNDERTAKEN ON OIL-BASED OR WATER-BASED PRIMERS AND BASE

COATS, AS WELL AS ON LACQUERED SURFACES. OMIT STEPS 1 AND 2 IF APPLYING OIL GILDING

TO ANY OF THESE SURFACES. APPLY GESSO (FOLLOWING STEPS 1 AND 2 OF THE WATER

GILDING INSTRUCTIONS) IF YOU WISH TO ACHIEVE OPTIMUM RESULTS, AS IT GIVES THE MOST

PERFECT SURFACE FOR GILDING. YOU MAY WANT TO PAINT A PRIMER OR BASE COAT ON TO

THE GESSO PRIOR TO OIL GILDING

1 If you want to gild only a small area when undertaking a design on furniture, use talc to produce a clean, dust-free and greaseproof surface. The talc will prevent the leaf from adhering to unsized areas, thus ensuring perfect accuracy. Put the talc in a pounce bag and wipe over the surface to give an even layer. Wipe off any excess talc with a soft brush, making sure that the talc is well rubbed in before painting on the size.

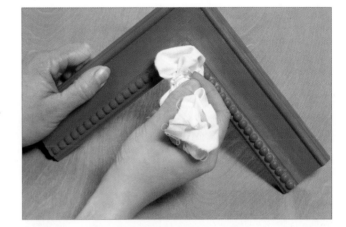

2 At this stage, you can use either water-based or oil-based size. Water-based size dries more quickly, becoming clear and tacky after 20 minutes. It can be tinted with watercolour for accurate application of the leaf. Apply a thin and even coat to the surface, avoiding air bubbles. Wash out the brushes using soap and water. Oil-based size comes in three types, which dry in 3, 12 or 24 hours. Drying times can be affected by atmosphere and climate but follow the instructions on the bottle. Oil-based size can be tinted with oil colours to produce a base tint. Apply a thin and even coat to the surface.

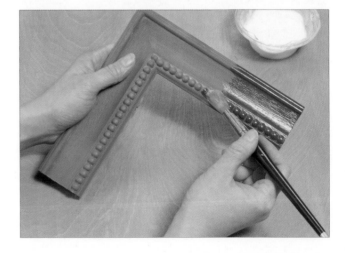

3 Use loose or transfer leaf. Open the book of leaf over a gilder's pad and blow the leaf on to the pad. You can cut the leaf into smaller pieces with a gilder's knife if required. Pick up some leaf with the knife and put it on the pad. Gently blow the leaf to make sure it is flat. Cut the leaf by drawing the blade towards you once.

4 To help in picking up the leaf, spread a little petroleum jelly on to your forearm and brush the gilder's tip over the jelly. Apply more jelly at frequent intervals. Using the tip, remove the leaf from the pad. Transfer leaf is applied with a short-bristled brush or your thumb by pressing down firmly after the leaf is held on to the size.

5 Lay the leaf on to the sized area using the tip. Each sheet of gold should overlap the next. Brush over with cotton wool (balls).

6 Any loose pieces or skewings can be brushed away with a soft brush and should be saved to be reused later.

7 Make sure the area is free of any loose gold, and seal with a wax or polish. Rub the polish on to the gilded area with a brush or by making a polishing rubber. Cover some wadding (batting) with a clean rag, leaving an opening at the top. Add a few drops of polish to soak the wadding. Close up the rag and when the liquid soaks through, start rubbing the gilded surface. The surface can be buffed up with a soft cloth when dry. Oil gilding can also be distressed using wire (steel) wool, fine sandpaper or a rag with a little white spirit (paint thinner). Always take care when distressing and don't rub too hard.

# $\mathscr{A}$LTERNATIVE METHODS

THERE IS A WIDE RANGE OF MATERIALS AVAILABLE NOW, THAT GIVE THE APPEARANCE OF GILDING, BUT AT A FRACTION OF THE PRICE. LIQUID LEAF, GOLD POWDERS, PASTES AND SPRAYS ARE AVAILABLE FROM MOST GOOD ART SUPPLIERS AND FRAMING SHOPS, AND COME IN A WIDE RANGE OF METALLIC HUES, FROM SILVER THROUGH TO ALL SHADES OF GOLD, COPPER AND BRONZE. LIQUID LEAF IS FAST DRYING AND EASY TO USE, WHILE GOLD SPRAYS SHOULD BE A BASIC MATERIAL IN ANY GILDER'S KIT. FRENCH ENAMEL VARNISH CAN BE USED ON ALL THESE MATERIALS ⌒

## LIQUID LEAF

1 Apply an oil- or water-based primer to the surface that is to be gilded and leave to dry. Paint on a base coat in the desired colour and leave to dry.

2 Shake the bottle of liquid leaf well and brush on to the surface with a real bristle brush or a gilding brush. Leave to dry, which usually takes about 20 minutes depending on the

brand. Seal with a varnish. The manufacturer will usually advise a sealant, but a polyurethane varnish or shellac will work.

## PASTES

1 Apply an oil- or water-based primer to the surface and leave to dry. Apply a base coat in the desired colour and leave to dry. This will enhance the final tone of the gold.

2 Apply the paste to the surface using a cloth or brush. Rub it in well, paying particular attention to any areas of detail. Leave to dry.

3 Rub the surface with a soft cloth, then seal with a wax or polish and polishing rubber if required.

## POWDERS

**1** Apply an oil- or water-based primer to the surface to be gilded and leave to dry. Paint on a base coat in the desired colour and leave to dry. The base colour will enhance the final tone of the gold. Apply oil- or water-based size and leave to become tacky.

**2** Place a little powder at a time on a saucer. Dip a brush into the powder, tapping off any excess, and brush it on to the size. Or, lift the loaded brush over the surface and gently blow the powder on to the size, making sure that the whole area is covered. Work in a ventilated area and at a distance from the powder. If covering a large surface, use the brush-on method and wear a mask.

**3** Seal with a polishing rubber or a coat of French enamel varnish. The colour of the varnish adds a jewel-like finish to the gold.

## PAINTS AND SPRAYS

**1** Apply an oil- or water-based primer to the surface and leave to dry. Paint or spray on a base coat in the desired colour and leave to dry. The base colour will enhance the final tone of the paint or spray.

**2** Shake the paint tin or spray can. If painting, paint an even coat on to the surface and leave to dry. Repeat if necessary. If spraying, work in a well-ventilated area and hold the can 30cm/12in from the surface. Spray an even coat all over. Leave to dry.

**3** Spray or paint does not need to be varnished but an amber shellac or coloured French enamel varnish will enhance the colour.

# $\mathcal{P}$REPARING SURFACES

PREPARING SURFACES FOR GILDING MUST BE DONE WELL IF THE END RESULT IS TO
BE AS SUCCESSFUL AS POSSIBLE. EACH TYPE OF SURFACE REQUIRES A DIFFERENT
PREPARATION. IT IS NOT WORTH SKIMPING ON THE PREPARATION STAGE WHEN
WORKING WITH REAL GOLD LEAF OR SOME OF THE OTHER MORE COSTLY
MATERIALS, AS THE RESULTS CAN BE VERY DISAPPOINTING AND EXPENSIVE ∽

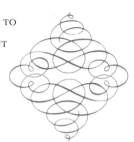

## GLASS AND CERAMICS

1 Wash and dry the glass thoroughly. If you are gilding
the whole surface, apply an acrylic primer and leave to
dry. If you are gilding a smaller design, mark this on the
glass and paint the area to be gilded with the primer.

2 Paint on a base coat of ceramic paint and leave to dry.
Sand lightly with fine sandpaper and dust off before
sizing. (If you are stencilling with gold paint, make sure
the paint is suitable for glass.)

## PLASTER

1 Make sure the surface is clean and dry. Seal with a coat
of PVA (white) glue and leave to dry. If the surface is old
and flaky, apply a coat of stabilizing primer.

2 Apply gesso or acrylic primer as required.

## METAL

1 If the metal is in poor condition, remove any dirt or rust with wire (steel) wool or with wet-and-dry sandpaper.

2 Apply the appropriate metal primer (in this case red oxide metal primer). Leave to dry before applying another colour if required.

## STONE

1 Make sure the surface is clean and dry. Seal with a coat of PVA (white) glue and leave to dry.

2 Apply acrylic primer. (It is not recommended to use real gold leaf on stone, so gesso is not required.)

## PLASTIC

1 Wash and dry the plastic. Fill any holes with car body repair filler. Sand with fine sandpaper and dust off.

2 Apply one coat of stabilizing primer and leave to dry, then apply one coat of acrylic primer.

# SPECIAL EFFECTS

THE PAINT FINISHES DESCRIBED IN THIS SECTION MAKE PERFECT BASES FOR MOST
GILDING TECHNIQUES. PREPARE ONE OF THE EFFECTS BELOW, THEN COMBINE
WITH GILDING FOR STUNNING RESULTS. THE FOUR PAINT FINISHES DESCRIBED ARE
SHOWN IN THE TRADITIONAL COLOURS, BUT TRY USING SOME MORE UNUSUAL
ONES FOR INTERESTING ALTERNATIVES ∽

## COLOURWASH

1 Apply one coat of acrylic wood primer to the surface and leave to dry.

2 Apply one coat of white or tinted emulsion (latex) paint to the primed surface and leave to dry.

3 In a container, mix six parts acrylic scumble glaze with one part emulsion or acrylic paint. Mix well.

4 Dip a dry brush into the glaze and apply to the surface using random strokes and allowing some of the base colour to show through. Leave to dry.

## TORTOISE-SHELL

1 Apply one coat of acrylic wood primer and leave to dry. Apply one coat of vinyl emulsion in a bamboo shade, or spray gold.

2 Mix a little acrylic scumble glaze and water with three shades of acrylic artist's colour: yellow-ochre, raw umber and burnt umber.

3 Using a separate brush for each colour, dab the paint on to the surface in a diagonal direction. Skim the surface with a softening brush to blend the colours.

4 Using a bristle brush, randomly spatter brown ink on to the surface to give the spotting often seen on tortoiseshell. Leave to dry and seal with varnishing wax or polish.

## LACQUER

1 Apply a synthetic gesso to the surface and leave to dry. Apply four or five more coats of gesso, leaving each coat to dry before applying the next, and sanding down between each coat.

2 Dilute some shellac with a little methylated spirit (methyl alcohol) and apply a single coat to the gesso. Leave to dry. Apply a coat of lacquer or gloss paint and leave to dry overnight.

3 Sand down with wet-and-dry sandpaper. Repeat this stage up to four times, sanding down after each coat of lacquer or gloss paint. The more coats applied, the better the finish and depth of colour will be.

4 Apply a coat of polyurethane varnish tinted with oil colour or a little lacquer or gloss. Leave to dry overnight.

## LAPIS LAZULI

1 Apply an oil-based undercoat and leave to dry. Apply an ultramarine-tinted low-odour eggshell paint and leave to dry overnight.

2 Mix one part ultramarine oil colour with two parts oil-based scumble glaze. Do the same with black oil colour. Dilute with white spirit (paint thinner) to make the consistency of single (light) cream. Apply these colours to the surface so that the ultramarine predominates with diagonal patches of black.

3 Gently skim over the surface with a softening brush to blend the colours into each other and eradicate the brush marks. Before the paint dries, dilute white, yellow-ochre and black oil colours with white spirit to make the consistency of single cream.

4 Using a separate brush for each colour, spatter over the wet surface in any order. Using a bristle brush, gently flick some bronze powder on to the surface to give the illusion of fool's gold. Leave to dry for 24 hours.

# FINISHING OFF

IT IS IMPORTANT TO SEAL YOUR PIECE PROPERLY AFTER GILDING, AS THIS WILL ENSURE THE LONG LIFE OF THE GILDING EFFECT. WHAT COULD BE MORE DISAPPOINTING THAN WATCHING YOUR LOVINGLY TRANSFORMED ITEMS DISTRESS WITH AGE? FOLLOW THE GUIDELINES FOR EACH DIFFERENT TECHNIQUE AND MATERIAL TO ENSURE THAT THE SEALANT YOU ARE USING IS RIGHT FOR THE JOB ∽

## POLISHING WITH SHELLAC

Using a brush or cloth, lightly cover the surface with the polish and leave to dry. Buff with a soft cloth.

## USING A POLISHING RUBBER

Cover some wadding (batting) with a clean rag. Add a few drops of polish to soak the wadding. Close up the rag and rub the gilded surface. Buff with a soft cloth when dry.

## AMBER SHELLAC VARNISH

Using a soft varnishing brush, apply a thin, even coat of amber shellac to the surface and leave to dry. This method will improve the gold tone of Dutch metal.

## FRENCH ENAMEL VARNISH

Using a soft varnishing brush, apply a thin, even coat of varnish to the surface. The different tones will enhance the look of substitute metallic effects.

## DISTRESSING

Gilding can be distressed before polishing or varnishing. Using wire (steel) wool on its own or dipped in a little methylated spirit (methyl alcohol), gently rub areas of detail or highlights. Rub only those areas that would receive wear naturally, so that the distressing does not look false. Fine sandpaper can also be used.

## SPATTERING

If you have distressed the gilding before sealing, a fine spattering of amber French enamel varnish may be used on areas of substitute leaf sealed with shellac or varnish. Use a stiff bristle brush and vary the size of dots by spattering from different distances from the surface.

## ℛESTORING

Restoring items is a most rewarding activity. Antique restoration requires great skill and if an item is very old or valuable, it is advisable to take it to a professional. If the item has been gilded in real gold leaf, make sure you match the carat as closely as possible. A good gilding sundries supplier should be able to help.

**Plaster**
Either mould and cast any missing sections yourself using latex or get a plaster workshop to do it for you. Using wet plaster or a recommended glue, insert the missing section and leave to dry. Seal it thoroughly and apply gesso or primer as required.

**Wood**
When restoring a wooden frame or table, fill any cracks and holes with putty or wood filler. Leave to dry and sand down, then apply gesso or primer as required. It is a difficult and costly undertaking to make accurate pieces for any missing sections of a wooden frame. Try using the method described for plaster and insert the piece using a recommended glue.

**Metal**
Replacing missing pieces on metal objects is best done by a qualified craftsperson. Remove any rust with wire (steel) wool or wet-and-dry sandpaper. Remove any heavy deposits with a wire brush and

detergent. Any cracks and holes that do not affect the structure can be filled with car body repair filler. Leave to dry and sand down. Prime with the appropriate metal primer.

**Conservation**
There are two ways of conserving antiques. The first is to restore them so that they do not look new but retain their naturally aged beauty. If an item is very old and valuable, the task is best left to a conservator. The second form of conservation is to make sure the item is kept in a place and atmosphere that will not affect its appearance or value, such as ensuring your pieces are not positioned in direct sunlight.

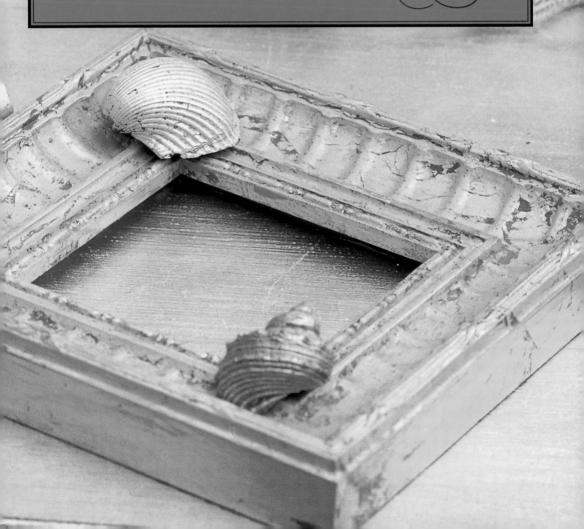

# THE GILDED ROOM

*Gilding, with its varying effects, is still one of the most popular forms of interior decoration and is indeed among the oldest. It improves with age and gives an immediate appearance of opulence.*

# OPULENT INTERIORS

ilding has been used in interior decoration for centuries. Gilded interiors immediately evoke the opulence of baroque and rococo salons, and the great palaces of Russia and France. The palace at Versailles was built for the glory of Louis XIV, and its gilded splendour was created as the antithesis of the gloomy palace at the Louvre. In Russia, astounding examples of gilded interiors

*Above: Take a cue from historic pieces when applying gilding. This chair has been lined with gilded decoration.*

survive, having withstood time and political turmoil. Splendid examples can be seen in Moscow, and in St Petersburg the Summer Palace remains as a remarkable examples of gilded interiors.

Today, many modern architects and furniture designers are experimenting with traditional and contemporary gilding effects, and gold detail can be used to great effect in historic and modern interiors alike. In your own home, you can try using traditional methods, or more adventurous touches, with materials such as composition leaf. Basic wooden items such as curtain poles and pelmets can be embellished with gold leaf, and combined with rich drapes of velvet, for a look of theatrical extravagance. Simple

*Left: Gilded details frame a doorway in the Palace at Ostankino, Moscow.*

*Above: The fabulously gilded bedroom of Louis XIV at Versailles.*

*Right: In the Peacock Room, originally designed by James MacNeil Whistler for a London house, art nouveau designs are enhanced by gilded finishes.*

modern pieces of furniture can be given the illusion of an antique by a clever application of distressed leaf, aged with acrylic varnish. Old junk shop finds can be given a new lease of life with such a treatment. Plaster and wooden architectural details can also be given the gold treatment, and can be a very cost-effective way of creating a feeling of historical classic grandeur.

# GILDED CHAIR

*An inexpensive Louis XIV-style wooden chair has*
*first been lacquered and then decorative details have*
*been applied in real gold leaf. The gilded chair*
*makes a luxurious centrepiece for your gilded room,*
*conjuring up images of the splendour of the court of*
*the Sun King at Versailles. Gild a single chair as a*
*focal point, or a whole set for real opulence* 〰

**YOU WILL NEED**

wooden Louis XIV-style
  chair frame
white acrylic primer
2.5cm/ l in paintbrushes
grey lacquer undercoat
dark green lacquer paint
cotton rags
talc
string
soft brush
water-based size

24-carat loose gold leaf
gilder's pad
gilder's knife
petroleum jelly
gilder's tip
cotton wool (balls)
burnishing brush or soft cloth
wire (steel) wool
methylated spirit (methyl
  alcohol)
wadding (batting)
transparent shellac polish

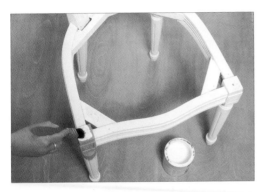

1 Prime the chair frame with acrylic primer and leave to dry for 1–2 hours.

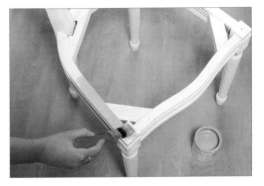

2 Paint on a coat of grey lacquer undercoat and leave to dry for 4 hours.

3 Paint on one or two coats of dark green lacquer paint and leave each coat to dry for at least 6–8 hours, or overnight if possible.

4 Fill a rag with talc and close up with string to make a pounce bag. Pounce the areas to be gilded and brush off the excess talc. ➤

5 Paint a thin, even coat of water-based size on to the areas to be gilded and leave for 20–30 minutes, until the size becomes clear and tacky.

6 Blow a sheet of gold leaf on to the gilder's pad, cut into small pieces with a gilder's knife if needed. Brush petroleum jelly on the inside of your arm and brush the gilder's tip over the jelly. Use the tip to pick up the leaf.

7 Lay the leaf on the sized area of the chair and gently press into place with cotton wool (balls). Continue until the whole sized area is covered with gold leaf.

8 Burnish with a burnishing brush or soft cloth to remove excess leaf. Dip some wire (steel) wool into methylated spirit (methyl alcohol) and rub gently on the detail to remove a little of the leaf. Take care not to rub too hard.

9 Make a polishing rubber by covering some wadding (batting) with a clean rag, leaving an opening at the top. Add a few drops of polish to soak the wadding. Close up the rag with string and when the liquid soaks through, start rubbing the gilded areas. The surface can be buffed up with a soft cloth when dry.

# RENAISSANCE FRAME

*This lovely antique-looking mirror with its*
*intricately moulded frame has been decorated using*
*the tricky but beautiful water gilding technique.*
*The delicate look of this type of gilding is ideal for*
*pieces of this kind and for restoring old frames to*
*their former glory* ∞

**YOU WILL NEED**

ready-made gesso in white
  and red
bain marie or double boiler
wooden picture frame
assorted bristle brushes
water-based size
24-carat loose gold leaf
gilder's pad
petroleum jelly
gilder's tip
cotton wool (balls)
agate burnisher
wire (steel) wool
wadding (batting)
cotton rag
transparent shellac polish
string

1 Heat the ready-made white gesso in a bain marie or double boiler for 5 minutes. Paint a coat of gesso on to the picture frame and leave to dry for 1–2 hours.

2 Heat the ready-made red gesso in the same way and paint up to eight coats of gesso on to the frame, leaving each to dry for 1–2 hours before applying the next.

3 Paint on a thin, even coat of water-based size and leave for 20–30 minutes, until it becomes clear and tacky.

4 Blow a sheet of gold leaf on to the gilder's pad. Brush some petroleum jelly on to the inside of your forearm and lightly brush the gilder's tip over the petroleum jelly. Use the tip to pick up the whole sheet. ➤

5 Lay the leaf on the frame and gently press into place with cotton wool (balls). Continue until the whole frame is covered.

6 Burnish with an agate burnisher to remove the excess leaf. Take care not to rub too hard as this will damage the gesso and spoil the finished effect.

7 To create a distressed effect in keeping with the antique appearance of the frame, gently rub the areas of detail with wire (steel) wool to remove a little of the leaf. Take care not to rub too hard.

8 Make a polishing rubber by covering some wadding (batting) with a clean rag, leaving an opening at the top. Add a few drops of polish to soak the wadding. Close up the rag with string and when the liquid soaks through, start rubbing the gilding. The surface can be buffed up with a soft cloth when dry.

# BEDSIDE TABLE

*This lovely little table has been decorated with real gold leaf using the versatile oil-gilding technique, which can be used to gild most surfaces. The delicate look of the piece has been retained by not gilding the entire table, but by concentrating on specific areas and details such as the top and the drawer knob*

**YOU WILL NEED**

small MDF (medium density fibreboard) bedside table
cotton rags
talc
string
soft brush
2.5cm/1 in paintbrush
water-based size
24-carat loose gold leaf
gilder's pad
gilder's knife
petroleum jelly
gilder's tip
soft 5cm/2in paintbrush
burnishing brush or soft cloth
wire (steel) wool
methylated spirit (methyl alcohol)
wadding (batting)
transparent shellac polish

1 Fill a cotton rag with talc and close up with string to make a pounce bag. Pounce the areas to be gilded and brush off excess talc with a soft brush. Paint a thin, even coat of water-based size on to the areas to be gilded and leave for 20–30 minutes, until clear and tacky. Blow a sheet of gold leaf on to the gilder's pad.

2 Brush some petroleum jelly on to the inside of your forearm and lightly brush the gilder's tip over the petroleum jelly. Use the tip to pick up the the whole sheet and lay it on the sized areas. Continue working in squares until the whole area is covered. Gently press into place with a soft paintbrush.

**3** Burnish the surface with a burnishing brush or soft cloth to remove the excess leaf until the table top is smooth. Dip some wire (steel) wool into a little methylated spirit (methyl alcohol) and rub gently over the surface and rim of the table to remove a little of the leaf. Take care not to rub too hard.

**4** Make a polishing rubber by covering some wadding (batting) with a clean rag, leaving an opening at the top. Add small drops of polish to soak the wadding. Close up the rag with string and when the liquid soaks through, start rubbing the gilded areas. The surface can be buffed up with a soft cloth when dry.

# SHELL FRAME

*Shells are ideal objects for gilding, which brings out their natural detail. Using them to adorn frames and mirrors gives the illusion of carvings reminiscent of the baroque interiors. In another context they can be used to transform a tired old bathroom or kitchen shelf*

**YOU WILL NEED**

assorted sea shells
red oxide spray primer
1.2cm/¹/₂ in bristle brushes
water-based size
Dutch metal leaf in gold and
  aluminium
burnishing brush or soft cloth
amber shellac and acrylic
  varnish
acrylic paints in pale blue,
  pink and orange
paint pans
soft cloths
gilded frame
PVA (white) glue

1 Spray the shells with an even coat of red oxide spray primer and leave to dry for 30 minutes to 1 hour.

2 Paint on a thin, even coat of water-based size and leave for 20–30 minutes, until it becomes clear and tacky.

3 Gild the shells with gold or aluminium Dutch metal leaf. Burnish with a burnishing brush or soft cloth to remove the excess leaf.

4 Seal the gold shells with a thin, even coat of amber shellac varnish and leave to dry for 45 minutes to 1 hour. Seal the aluminium shells with acrylic varnish and leave to dry for 1 hour.

5 Mix some pale blue acrylic paint with a little water. Paint on to the shells, then rub off most of the paint with a cloth, allowing only a little paint to remain in the areas of detail. Colour some of the shells in pink and orange. Leave to dry for 30 minutes.

6 Arrange the shells on the gilded frame and attach with PVA glue. Leave to dry thoroughly before hanging in place.

# WOODEN DRAWER KNOBS

*These plain and simple wooden knobs have been decorated with two gilding techniques, both using inexpensive gold composite Dutch metal. The first technique gives the knobs a distressed look, while the second imitates rust*

**YOU WILL NEED**

wooden drawer or door knobs
red oxide spray primer
2.5cm/1in paintbrush
water-based size
broken gold Dutch metal leaf
    (schlag) or gold Dutch metal
    leaf
burnishing brush or soft cloth
water-based matt varnish
paint pans
powder pigment in burnt
    umber and yellow-ochre
bristle brushes
amber shellac varnish
    (optional)
1.2cm/¹/₂in varnishing brush
    (optional)

1 Working in a well-ventilated area, spray the knobs with red oxide spray primer. Leave to dry for 1 hour.

2 Paint on a thin, even coat of water-based size and leave for 20–30 minutes, until it becomes clear and tacky.

3 Gild the knobs by sprinkling broken gold Dutch metal leaf on the surface. Burnish with a burnishing brush or soft cloth to remove excess leaf and bring up the lustre.

4 Alternatively, gild the knobs with sheets of gold Dutch metal leaf to cover the entire area. Burnish with a burnishing brush or soft cloth to remove any loose leaf and bring up the lustre. Pour some water-based varnish into two paint pans.

5 Add burnt umber pigment to one pan and yellow-ochre pigment to the other. Using a separate brush for each colour, dab on patches of the two colours to build up the rust effect, allowing some of the gold to show through. Leave to dry for 1–2 hours.

6 The use of varnish with the pigment will seal the surface, so there is no need for further sealing, but you can apply a thin, even coat of amber shellac varnish if you wish. Leave to dry for 1 hour.

# PLASTER CORBEL

*This baroque-style plaster corbel has been decorated*
*using the water-gilding technique to retain the beauty*
*of the architectural detail. Plaster pieces like this one*
*are available from specialist suppliers who can help*
*when you need replacements at home*

**YOU WILL NEED**

| | |
|---|---|
| plaster corbel | 24-carat loose gold leaf |
| PVA (white) glue | cotton (wool) balls |
| 2.5cm/1 in paintbrush | agate burnisher |
| ready-made red gesso | wire (steel) wool |
| bain marie or double boiler | wadding (batting) |
| methylated spirit (methyl alcohol) | cotton rag |
| jar | transparent shellac polish |
| acrylic bristle brush | string |

**1** Mix two parts PVA (white) glue with one part water and use to seal the corbel. Leave to dry for 2 hours. Heat the gesso in a bain marie or double boiler. Paint the corbel with eight coats of gesso, leaving it to dry for 1-2 hours between coats.

**2** Make some gilding water by adding a little methylated spirit (methyl alcohol) to some water in a jar until the water is slightly coloured. Paint a small area of the corbel with the gilding water.

**3** Working with one piece at a time, lay each piece of gold leaf carefully on the damp surface, pressing gently into place with cotton (wool) balls. Work the leaf well into the areas of detail.

**4** Continue painting small areas with gilding water and applying gold leaf until it is covered. Burnish with an agate burnisher. Do not damage the gesso underneath.

**5** Distress the surface by gently rubbing with wire (steel) wool, taking care not to rub too hard. Concentrate on the areas in relief, to simulate natural wear and tear.

**6** Cover some wadding (batting) with a clean rag. Add a few drops of polish to soak the wadding. Tie the rag with string and when the liquid soaks through, rub the surface.

# LAMP BASE

*This simple ceramic lamp base is gilded in three colours of Dutch metal leaf to give it a contemporary feel that would lend itself to a modern interior. It is then enhanced with a verdigris paint finish. Gild a lampshade to match* ⌒

**YOU WILL NEED**

ceramic lamp base
masking tape
sandpaper
white acrylic primer
2.5cm/1 in paintbrushes
dark green emulsion (latex) paint
water-based size
pencil (optional)

Dutch metal leaf in silver, gold and copper
burnishing brush or soft cloth
wire (steel) wool
methylated spirit (methyl alcohol)
water-based varnishing wax
viridian-green acrylic paint
soft cloth

1 Mask off the fittings and lead with masking tape and sand down the surface of the lamp base to provide a key for the paint to adhere to.

2 Prime the base with white acrylic primer and leave to dry for 1–2 hours. Paint the base with two coats of dark green emulsion, leaving each coat to dry for 2–3 hours.

3 Paint a thin coat of water-based size on the top section of the base. (Draw a guide line if necessary.) Leave for 20–30 minutes, until the size becomes clear and tacky.

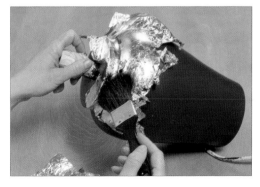

4 Gild the top section of the base with silver Dutch metal leaf. Burnish the surface with a burnishing brush or soft cloth to remove the excess leaf.  ➤

5 Dip some wire (steel) wool into a little methylated spirit (methyl alcohol) and gently rub to distress the surface.

6 Size the bottom half of the base and leave for 20–30 minutes to become clear and tacky.

7 Gently crush the gold and copper leaf in your hands and apply randomly over the surface, allowing plenty of base coat to show through. When the surface is covered, burnish with a burnishing brush or soft cloth.

8 Distress the bottom half of the base with wire wool dipped in a little methylated spirit.

9 Seal the entire surface with a thin, even coat of varnishing wax and leave to dry for 1 hour.

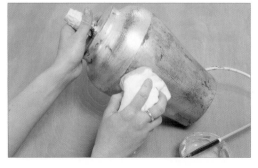

10 Mix viridian-green paint with a little water and paint on to the surface. Rub off most of the paint with a cloth.

# ℙLASTER  DECORATIONS

*Decorating a plain wall with plaster shapes is
unusual in itself but adding gilding to the shapes
will make them even more stunning and
individual. The shapes can be applied directly to a
wall, or on small decorative panels or doors* ☜

| YOU WILL NEED | |
|---|---|
| plaster shapes | plumbline |
| PVA (white) glue | acrylic paints in yellow-ochre |
| assorted decorator's brushes | and rose |
| waterproof ceramic adhesive | acrylic scumble glaze |
| masking tape | paint pans |
| white acrylic wood primer | water-based size |
| white emulsion (latex) paint | gold Dutch metal leaf |
| ruler | burnishing brush or soft cloth |
| | water-based varnishing wax |

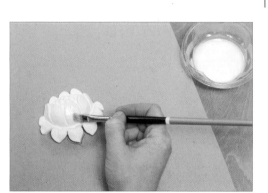

1 Mix two parts PVA (white) glue with one part water
and seal the plaster shapes with this mixture, working the
sealant into the recesses. Leave to dry for 2 hours.

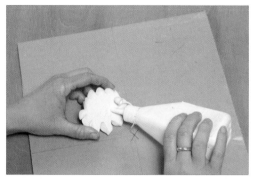

2 Use a thick, even coat of ceramic adhesive to stick the
shapes on to the panel. Leave to dry for 3–4 hours. Hold
the shapes in place with masking tape while the glue is
drying, if necessary.

3 Paint the panel and shapes with a coat of white acrylic
primer and leave to dry for 1–2 hours. Paint on a coat of
white emulsion (latex) and leave to dry for 2–3 hours.

4 Measure out the positions of the stripes on the panel. Use
a ruler to mark the first stripe with masking tape. Reduce
the tackiness of the tape on a piece of cloth first.    ➤

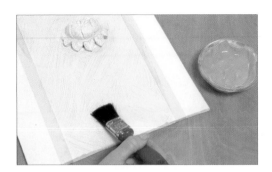

**5** Mix one part yellow-ochre acrylic paint with six parts scumble glaze. Apply to the area between the masking tape using random brush strokes and allowing plenty of the base colour to show through the glaze. Leave to dry.

**6** Remove the masking tape and remask along the outside edge of the glazed stripe. Mix one part rose acrylic paint with six parts scumble glaze. Paint the second stripe in the same way as the first and leave to dry for 2–3 hours.

**7** Paint a thin, even coat of water-based size on to the plaster shapes, working it into the recesses, and leave for 20–30 minutes, until it becomes clear and tacky.

**8** Place a sheet of gold Dutch metal leaf on to the sized surface and press lightly into the detail, smoothing with your fingers and ensuring that the whole shape is covered.

**9** Burnish the shapes with a burnishing brush or soft cloth to remove the excess leaf.

**10** Seal with a thin, even coat of water-based varnishing wax and leave to dry.

# CORNER CUPBOARD

*This gothic-style wooden corner cupboard has been gilded using aluminium Dutch metal leaf on a blue base coat. The cupboard retains its historical feel and the gilding process creates the illusion of steel, creating a timeless yet contemporary piece*

**YOU WILL NEED**

| | |
|---|---|
| wooden corner cupboard | wire (steel) wool |
| royal-blue emulsion (latex) paint | methylated spirit (methyl alcohol) |
| 2.5cm/1 in paintbrushes | water-based flat varnish |
| water-based size | viridian-green acrylic paint |
| aluminium Dutch metal leaf | paint pan |
| burnishing brush or soft cloth | soft cloth |

**1** Paint the cupboard in royal-blue emulsion (latex), making sure the whole surface and any details are well covered, and leave to dry for 2–3 hours. Apply a second coat and leave to dry.

**2** Paint on a thin, even coat of water-based size and leave for 20–30 minutes, until it becomes clear and tacky.

**3** Gild the cupboard with aluminium Dutch metal leaf, making sure the whole surface is covered. Burnish with a burnishing brush or soft cloth to remove the excess leaf.

**4** Dip some wire (steel) wool into a little methylated spirit (methyl alcohol) and lightly rub the edges and areas of detail to reveal some of the base coat beneath the aluminium leaf. Seal with water-based flat varnish and leave to dry for about 3 hours.

**5** Mix some viridian-green acrylic paint with a little water and paint on to the surface. Working quickly, rub off most of the paint with a soft cloth, leaving only a little paint in the areas of detail. Use a clean area of cloth each time or you will rub the colour back on.

# STENCILLED HEART CUSHION

*A simple cushion can be transformed by stencilling with fabric paints to make a uniquely individual accessory. A collection of cushions, all slightly different but made on the same theme, will brighten up your sitting room or bedroom*

**YOU WILL NEED**

| | |
|---|---|
| fabric squares, 46cm/18in | cutting mat |
| masking tape | drawing pins |
| gold fabric paint | iron |
| small paintbrush | needle and matching thread |
| pencil | 30cm/12in zipper |
| paper | cushion pad, 30cm/12in |
| stencil cardboard | square |
| craft knife | 2m/2yd fringing |

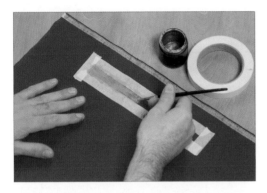

1 Mask off a border on one fabric square with masking tape. Each edge should be approximately 23cm/9in long and 1.2cm/½in wide, with a gap at each corner for the heart motif. Apply two coats of fabric paint between the masked areas, leaving the first coat to dry thoroughly before applying the next.

2 Trace the small heart template from the back of the book and transfer to four pieces of stencil cardboard. Cut out four hearts with a craft knife on a cutting mat. Using drawing pins, pin them in place in the gaps in the border so that they point towards the centre. Apply two coats of fabric paint through each stencil, leaving the first coat to dry thoroughly before applying the next.

3 Trace the large heart template from the back of the book and cut from stencil cardboard. Pin firmly in the centre of the fabric. Apply three coats of gold fabric paint, allowing each coat to dry thoroughly before applying the next. Using a hot iron, press the wrong side of the fabric to fix the paint. Make up the cushion, insert the zipper and cushion pad and decorate with fringing.

# APPLIQUÉ STAR CUSHION

*This sumptuous cushion is quite simple to make. It uses an appliqué technique, with the pieces first painted with gold fabric paint. The bold design would complement any interior and makes a beautifully individual gift. The simple yet effective shapes could be repeated on a throw or the border of a curtain, or even stencilled in gold on a wall* ∞

**YOU WILL NEED**

pencil
craft knife
cutting mat
cardboard
1m/1yd white canvas
gold fabric paint
small paintbrush
iron
scissors
fabric glue
2 blue fabric squares, 25cm/10in
2 burgundy fabric squares, 25cm/10in
button blank
sewing machine
matching threads
fabric square, 46cm/18in, for the back
30cm/12in zipper
cushion pad, 30cm/12in square
2m/2yd fringing

1 Trace the star template from the back of the book. Using a craft knife on a cutting mat, cut out a star from cardboard. Draw around the cardboard template four times on canvas.

2 Paint the stars and a small gold circle for covering the button with two coats of gold fabric paint. Using a hot iron, press the wrong side of the canvas to fix the paint, then cut out the stars and circle.

3 Using fabric glue, stick a star into the centre of each of the four fabric squares and leave to dry. Cover the button blank with the gold circle.

4 Sew around the stars with a zigzag stitch. Sew the squares together. Make up the cushion, insert the zipper and pad, and sew on the fringing and the button.

# Curtain pole and pelmet

*Simple medium density fibreboard pelmets and plain wooden curtain poles are radically transformed by gilding. As they are quite large, using Dutch metal leaf will considerably reduce the cost of the project. Try experimenting with combinations of the available colours to create different effects*

**YOU WILL NEED**

plain wooden curtain pole and rings
red oxide spray primer
water-based size
assorted decorator's brushes
Dutch metal leaf in copper, aluminium and gold
burnishing brush or soft cloth
acrylic varnishing wax
plain MDF (medium density fibreboard) pelmet
red oxide paint
wire (steel) wool
methylated spirit (methyl alcohol)
amber shellac varnish
red acrylic paint
paint pan
soft cloth

## Curtain pole

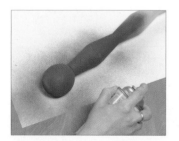

**1** Spray an even coat of red oxide primer over the curtain pole and rings and leave to dry for 1 hour.

**2** Paint a thin coat of water-based size on to the sections of the pole to be gilded in copper. Leave for 20–30 minutes, until clear and tacky.

**3** Gild the sized areas with copper Dutch metal leaf. Burnish with a burnishing brush or cloth to remove the excess leaf.

**4** Size the remaining sections of the pole and leave for 20–30 minutes, until the size becomes clear and tacky.

**5** Gild with aluminium Dutch metal leaf and burnish with a burnishing brush or cloth to remove the excess leaf.

**6** Seal the curtain pole with two coats of acrylic varnishing wax. Leave to dry for 2–3 hours between each coat. ➤

## PELMET

1 Prime the pelmet with a coat of red oxide paint and leave to dry for 2–3 hours.

2 Apply a thin, even coat of water-based size and leave for 20–30 minutes, until it becomes clear and tacky.

3 Gild the surface with gold Dutch metal leaf. Use a burnishing brush or soft cloth to remove the excess leaf.

4 Dip some wire (steel) wool into a little methylated spirit (methyl alcohol). Gently rub the edges to wear slightly.

5 Seal with a thin, even coat of amber shellac varnish and leave to dry for 45 minutes to 1 hour. Mix some red acrylic paint with a little water. Paint on to the surface and leave to set for 5 minutes.

6 Rub off most of the paint with a cloth, allowing only a little to remain in the areas of detail. Dampen the cloth if the paint has set too much. Leave to dry.

# TASSELS AND TIE-BACKS

*Here is another unusual way of decorating your windows with gilding. Rope and jute tie-backs are widely available and using gold Dutch metal leaf and metallic sprays to gild them is an inexpensive way to add glamour to curtains and upholstery* ∽

**YOU WILL NEED**
jute tie-back
5cm/2in paintbrush
water-based size
large bucket
PVA (white) glue
red oxide spray primer
2.5cm/1in paintbrushes
gold Dutch metal leaf
burnishing brush or soft cloth
amber shellac varnish
jute tassel
copper spray paint

1 Paint the tie-back liberally with water-based size and a 5cm/2in brush and leave to drain off in a large bucket overnight. Repeat the process and leave to drain and dry again overnight. Dilute two parts PVA (white) glue with one part water in a large bucket and stir well.

2 Paint the tie-back liberally with the glue mixture, dunking it into the bucket if necessary to make sure it is completely soaked. Discard the PVA mixture and leave the tie-back to drain off over the now empty bucket in a warm place overnight. When dry, the tie-back should be quite hard and crispy.

3 Prime the tie-back with red oxide spray primer, making sure that the whole area and any recesses are covered. Leave to dry for 30 minutes to 1 hour.

4 Using a 2.5cm/1in brush, paint water-based size over the tie-back, trying to get into all the cracks but avoiding too many bubbles. Leave for 20–30 minutes, until the size becomes tacky. ➤

**5** Gild the tie-back with gold Dutch metal leaf, getting into as much of the detail as possible. Burnish with a burnishing brush or soft cloth to remove the excess leaf.

**6** Seal the tie-back with a thin, even coat of amber shellac varnish and leave to dry for 30 minutes to 1 hour.

**7** Spray the tassel with copper paint, making sure that all the tufts at the base are covered. Leave to dry for 30 minutes and repeat.

**8** Paint the top of the tassel with water-based size and leave for 20–30 minutes, until tacky and clear. Gild the top of the tassel and remove excess leaf with your fingers.

**9** Paint the top of the tassel with a thin, even coat of amber shellac varnish and leave to dry for 30 minutes to 1 hour.

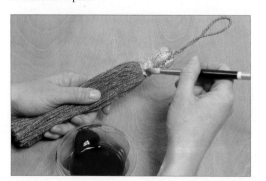

# ℬATHROOM ACCESSORIES

*This very decadent use of gilding will add an atmosphere of richness and glamour to your bathroom. Using gold Dutch metal leaf is an inexpensive way of transforming cheap basic accessories to make your smallest room into a glittering haven* ⌀

**YOU WILL NEED**

plain wooden toilet seat
plain wooden towel rail
plain wooden toilet roll holder
sandpaper
white acrylic wood primer
2.5cm/1in paintbrushes
red oxide spray primer
water-based size
gold Dutch metal leaf
burnishing brush or soft cloth
wire (steel) wool
methylated spirit (methyl alcohol)
water-based acrylic varnish
gold tassels

1 Sand off any coating on the wood of the toilet seat and accessories to provide a key for the paint. Prime the surfaces with acrylic wood primer and leave to dry for 1–2 hours.

2 Spray an even coat of red oxide primer over the toilet seat and accessories, making sure all the surfaces are evenly coated. Leave to dry for 1 hour.

3 Paint a thin coat of water-based size on the entire surface of the toilet seat and leave for 20–30 minutes, until the size becomes clear and tacky.

4 Gild the entire surface of the toilet seat with gold Dutch metal leaf. Burnish with a burnishing brush or soft cloth to remove the excess leaf. ➤

**5** Dip some wire (steel) wool into a little methylated spirit (methyl alcohol) and gently rub the edges to appear as natural wear. Seal the surface with water-based acrylic varnish and leave to dry.

**6** Size the towel rail and toilet roll holder and leave for 20–30 minutes, until the size becomes clear and tacky.

**7** Gild the accessories with gold Dutch metal leaf and burnish.

**8** Distress the accessories with wire wool and methylated spirit.

**9** Seal with water-based acrylic varnish. Hang gold tassels from the ends of the accessories to add extra glamour.

# ℋ ERALDIC TILES

*Tiles are a joy to gild as the ceramic surface is so*
*smooth. This is a quick and easy way of creating a*
*luxurious decor in your bathroom or kitchen or of*
*rejuvenating existing tiles. Sealing the tiles after*
*gilding makes them hard-wearing and waterproof,*
*so that they will look wonderful for years* ∞

**YOU WILL NEED**
ceramic tiles
stencil cardboard
pencil
craft knife
cutting mat
masking tape
soft cloths
water-based size
2.5cm/1in paintbrushes

Dutch metal leaf in aluminium,
  copper and gold
burnishing brush or soft cloth
stencil brush
water-based varnishing wax
  or flat varnish

1 Trace the crown and fleur-de-lys templates from the
back of the book and transfer on to the stencil cardboard.
Use a craft knife to cut out the stencils on a cutting mat.

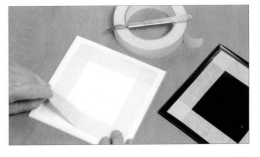

2 Reduce the tackiness of the masking tape on a piece of
cloth, then mask off the border on the tiles.

3 You can prime the tiles if desired, but a pleasing effect is
created by allowing the colour of the tiles to show
through. To gild a whole tile, paint a thin, even coat of
water-based size over the entire surface and leave for
20–30 minutes, until it becomes tacky.

4 Crush some aluminium Dutch metal leaf gently in your
hand and apply randomly to the surface, so that some of
the tile shows through. Burnish with a burnishing brush
or soft cloth to remove the excess leaf, taking care not to
rub too hard.                                    ➤

**5** To gild the borders, paint a coat of size around the edge of the tile, up to the masking tape. Leave the size for 20–30 minutes until it becomes tacky and clear.

**6** Place a stencil in the centre of the tile. Using a stencil brush, stipple water-based size through the stencil. Leave for 20–30 minutes until it becomes tacky and clear.

**7** Gild the fleur-de-lys design and borders with copper Dutch metal leaf. Burnish with a burnishing brush or soft cloth to remove the excess leaf, taking care not to rub too hard.

**8** Gild the crown design and borders with gold Dutch metal leaf. Burnish with a burnishing brush or soft cloth to remove the excess leaf, taking care not to rub too hard.

**9** Seal the tiles with water-based varnishing wax or flat varnish. If using wax, leave to dry for 1 hour, then buff with a cloth. If using varnish, you may need to apply two coats, allowing 2 hours drying time between each coat.

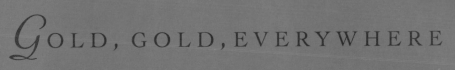

# GOLD, GOLD, EVERYWHERE

*Gilding does not have to be confined to traditional objects. It can be used on many different surfaces, and will give the most unassuming and inexpensive item a new lease of life.*

# DECORATIVE ITEMS

*J*ust one gilded item in a room can create a touch of glamour. Almost anything can be gilded, so scour junk shops and flea markets for supposed lost causes, and see how fantastic the results can be. Mass-produced items can also be given an individual touch – a simple candlestick is the perfect candidate for the gold treatment. As candlesticks, both traditional and modern, are available in interesting shapes they provide a wonderful surface to work upon. Small items also allow you the liberty of trying out different gilding effects – whether you are aiming for a classic result, or a contemporary look. Transform a simple wooden or cardboard box with gold leaf, powders or pastes, to create a glorious gift box or storage box for precious secrets.

With new materials arriving on the market, you can create the look without using the more lengthy, traditional methods, making gilding easier and quicker to achieve than ever before. The key is to be imaginative – and brave – when considering what to gild. No matter how unlikely the object first seems, keep your eyes open to the potential of the technique, and go for gold.

*Above: A carved wooden frame is gilded with Dutch metal leaf, then embellished with tassels and plaster decorations.*

*Right: Gold powder was used to decorate this sun-burst mirror.*

*Below: Aluminium leaf adds lustre to a wooden candlestick.*

*Above: Strong, contemporary shapes are the perfect foil for gilding.*

# PLANT URN

*It is hard to believe that this beautiful piece came from humble beginnings, but it started life as a simple plastic plant urn. The use of Dutch metal leaf makes the urn inexpensive to gild, and the technique makes it easy to produce an item of beauty that you won't want to keep outdoors*

**YOU WILL NEED**

plastic plant urn
sandpaper
red oxide spray primer
water-based size
assorted bristle brushes
gold Dutch metal leaf
burnishing brush or soft cloth
wire (steel) wool
methylated spirit (methyl
   alcohol)
amber shellac varnish
acrylic paints in pale blue
   and grey
paint pan
soft cloth

1 Sand the surface of the urn to provide a key for the paint to adhere to. Spray with red oxide spray primer and leave to dry.

2 Paint on a thin, even coat of water-based size and leave for 20–30 minutes, until it becomes clear and tacky.

3 Carefully lay the gold Dutch metal leaf on to the surface to cover the whole area. Burnish with a burnishing brush or soft cloth to remove the excess leaf and bring up the lustre.

4 Dip some wire (steel) wool into a little methylated spirit (methyl alcohol) and gently rub the raised areas and details of the urn to distress the surface, taking care not to rub too hard.

5 Seal with a thin, even coat of amber shellac varnish and leave to dry for 45 minutes to 1 hour.

6 Mix the blue and grey acrylic paint with a little water. Paint the surface and leave to set for 5 minutes. Rub off most of the paint with a cloth, allowing only a little paint to remain in the areas of detail. Dampen the cloth if the paint has set too much. Leave to dry.

# LAMPSHADE

*A simple parchment lampshade makes an ideal base for gilding. This stencilled design on a shellac base coat gives the shade an antique appearance. Remember always to use a low-wattage bulb with this shade to avoid tarnishing*

**YOU WILL NEED**

plain parchment lampshade
stencil brushes
amber shellac varnish
pencil
stencil cardboard
craft knife
cutting mat
masking tape
gold stencil
paint

**1** Using a large round stencil brush, stipple an even but blotchy coat of amber shellac varnish over the surface of the lampshade and leave to dry for 30 minutes to 1 hour.

**2** Trace the templates from the back of the book and transfer on to stencil cardboard.

**3** Cut out the stencils with a craft knife on a cutting mat. It is easier if you move the stencil towards the blade when cutting.

**4** Mark the positions for the stencils around the lampshade. Secure the first stencil at the bottom of the shade with masking tape. Stir the gold paint well, then stipple through the stencil. Do not load the brush with too much paint or it will bleed. Remove the stencil carefully before repositioning the next one.

**5** When you have completed the bottom row, secure the second stencil at the top of the shade with masking tape. Stencil the top row in the same way as before and leave the shade to dry for at least 1 hour before using.

# HEAD OF MARS

*Plaster copies of details from famous statues are now widely available and are relatively inexpensive, as well as being easy to gild. This head of Mars has been gilded using copper Dutch metal leaf. The gilding was then enhanced with a verdigris finish to give an antique appearance*

**YOU WILL NEED**

plaster head
PVA (white) glue
2.5cm/1 in paintbrushes
deep red acrylic gesso
water-based size
copper Dutch metal leaf
burnishing brush or soft cloth
wire (steel) wool
methylated spirit (methyl alcohol)
water-based varnishing wax
acrylic paints in deep green, viridian-green, yellow-ochre and white
paint palette
bristle brushes
old sheet or towel
flower mister
whiting (French chalk)
flat acrylic transparent varnish

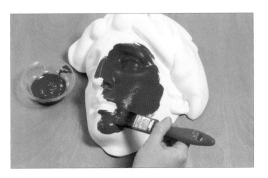

1 Seal the head with a mixture of PVA (white) glue diluted with one part water. Leave to dry for 2–3 hours. Prime the head with a coat of deep red acrylic gesso and leave to dry for 2 hours.

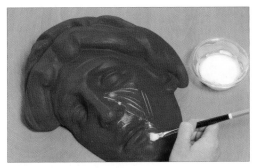

2 Paint on a thin coat of water-based size and leave for 20–30 minutes, until it becomes clear and tacky.

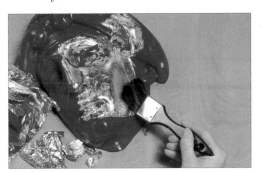

3 Lay copper leaf on to the sized head until the whole surface is covered. Burnish with a burnishing brush or soft cloth to remove excess leaf and smooth the surface.

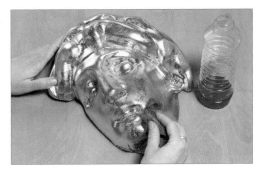

4 Dip some wire wool into a little methylated spirit (methyl alcohol) and gently rub the surface to reveal some of the base coat.                         ➤

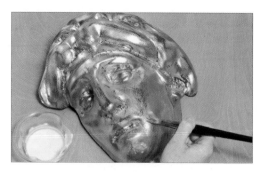

**5** Paint a thin, even coat of water-based varnishing wax on to the surface and leave to dry for 1–2 hours.

**6** To make a verdigris colour, mix some deep green and viridian-green acrylic paint with water on a palette. Separately mix some yellow-ochre and white acrylic paint with a little water.

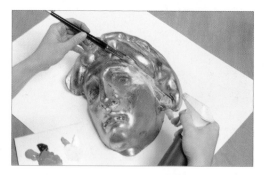

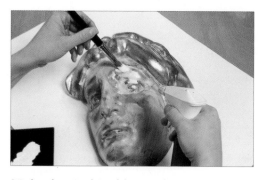

**7** Place the head on a sheet or towel. Dab the verdigris mix on to the surface. Working quickly, spray water from the flower mister over the paint to disperse it and so that it dribbles down the head. Dab some off-white colour into the details and disperse with water again.

**8** Before the paint dries, dab some whiting (French chalk) into the areas of detail where it will adhere to the damp paint. Brush away any excess whiting and leave the head to dry for 2 hours.

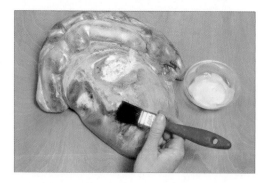

**9** Paint the entire surface with acrylic varnish, taking care to cover any recesses and details and leave to dry for 1–2 hours.

# GILDED VASE

*Glass is a lovely surface for gilding and frosted glass is especially suitable as its slightly rough surface provides the perfect key for size. If you are planning to decorate glasses used for drinking, it is not advisable to gild them* ∞

**YOU WILL NEED**

frosted glass vase
2.5cm/1 in paintbrush
water-based size
Dutch metal leaf in copper
  and silver
burnishing brush or soft cloth
pencil
stencil cardboard

craft knife
cutting mat
stencil brush
water-based varnishing wax
soft cloth

1 Paint a thin coat of water-based size on to the rim and near the bottom edge of the vase. Leave for 20–30 minutes, until it becomes clear and tacky. Usually a coat of primer is applied before the size but for this vase it has been omitted to achieve a more delicate look. The vase will wear just as well once sealed.

2 Gild the sized areas with copper Dutch metal leaf. Burnish with a burnishing brush or soft cloth to remove the excess leaf, but be careful not to rub too hard.

3 Trace the template from the back of the book and transfer to stencil cardboard. Cut out with a craft knife on a cutting mat.

4 Place the stencil on the vase and stipple through water-based size with a stencil brush. Remove the stencil and leave the size for 20–30 minutes, until clear and tacky. ➢

**5** Gild the stencilled crosses with silver Dutch metal leaf and burnish with a burnishing brush or soft cloth.

**6** Seal the gilded areas with water-based varnishing wax and leave to dry for about 1 hour. Polish with a soft cloth to bring up the lustre.

# CANDLESTICK

*Candlesticks are available in many different shapes and sizes. They can be given a rich, aged effect with the use of the various shades of Dutch metal leaf. Don't forget to look for candlesticks in junk shops, where you may find more unusual pieces* ∽

**YOU WILL NEED**

wooden candlestick
red oxide spray primer
water-based size
assorted bristle brushes
gold Dutch metal leaf
burnishing brush or soft cloth
wire (steel) wool
methylated spirit (methyl alcohol)
amber shellac varnish
acrylic paints in red and yellow-ochre
paint pan
soft cloth

**1** Spray the candlestick with an even coat of red oxide spray primer, making sure all the details and recesses are covered. Leave to dry for 30 minutes to 1 hour.

**2** Paint on a thin, even coat of water-based size and leave for 20–30 minutes, until it becomes clear and tacky.

**3** Carefully lay the gold Dutch metal leaf on to the surface to cover the whole area. Burnish with a burnishing brush or soft cloth to remove the excess leaf and bring up the lustre.

**4** Dip some wire (steel) wool into a little methylated spirit (methyl alcohol) and gently rub the raised areas and details of the candlestick to distress the surface, taking care not to rub too hard.

**5** Seal with a thin, even coat of amber shellac varnish and leave to dry for 45 minutes to 1 hour.

**6** Mix the red and yellow-ochre acrylic paint with a little water. Paint on to the surface and leave to set for 5 minutes. Rub off most of the paint with a cloth, allowing only a little paint to remain in the areas of detail. Dampen the cloth if the paint has set too much. Leave to dry.

# PLANT POTS

*Ordinary terracotta plant pots are pleasing objects in themselves and can be decorated in many ways. Gilded plant pots make attractive bases for fresh or dried flower arrangements. They can also be used for holding candles, which can be secured with florists' foam*

**YOU WILL NEED**

assorted terracotta plant pots
red oxide spray primer
water-based size
2.5cm/1 in bristle brushes
gold Dutch metal leaf
burnishing brush or soft cloth
wire (steel) wool
methylated spirit
(methyl alcohol)
amber shellac varnish
blue acrylic paint
paint pan
soft cloth

1 Remove any earth or grit and wash the pots well. Leave to dry. Spray with red oxide primer and leave to dry for 30 minutes to 1 hour.

2 Paint on a thin, even coat of water-based size and leave for 20–30 minutes, until it becomes clear and tacky.

3 Carefully lay pieces of Dutch metal leaf on to the surfaces over the entire area. Burnish with a burnishing brush or soft cloth to remove the excess leaf and bring up the lustre.

4 Dip some wire (steel) wool into a little methylated spirit (methyl alcohol) and gently rub the pots along the rims and areas where they would suffer wear and tear. Take care not to rub too hard. Seal with an even coat of amber shellac varnish and leave to dry for 45 minutes to 1 hour.

5 Mix some blue acrylic paint with a little water. Paint on to the surface and allow to set for 5 minutes. Rub off most of the paint with a cloth, so that only a little paint remains in areas of detail. Dampen the cloth if the paint has set too much.

# AMPHORA

*This amphora, bought from a garden centre, has been decorated using gilding and a lapis lazuli paint effect to give it an ancient feel. The dotting of amber shellac over the amphora creates the illusion of rust on the surface. The deep ultramarine is reminiscent of the colour favoured by the ancient Egyptians*

**YOU WILL NEED**

terracotta amphora
pale blue spray paint
acrylic paints in ultramarine, black, white, yellow-ochre and viridian-green
texture gel
paint pans
large, round stencil brush
pencil (optional)
water-based size
2.5cm/1in paintbrushes
gold Dutch metal leaf
burnishing brush or soft cloth
water-based varnishing wax
soft cloths
fine and stiff-bristle paintbrushes
amber French enamel varnish
flower mister
old sheet or towel
water-based matt (flat) acrylic varnish

1 Wash the amphora, if necessary, and leave to dry. Spray with an even coat of pale blue spray paint, making sure that the whole area is covered. Leave to dry for 1 hour.

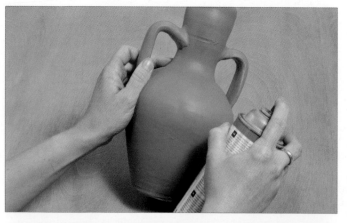

2 Mix some ultramarine acrylic paint with some texture gel. Using a large, round stencil brush, stipple a heavy coat around the bottom half of the amphora. Draw a line around the middle of the amphora if necessary. Leave to dry for 3 hours. The paint should have a hard texture when dry.

**3** Paint a thin coat of water-based size on to the top half of the amphora, making sure that the whole area is covered. Leave for 20–30 minutes, until clear and tacky.

**4** Gild the sized areas with gold Dutch metal leaf. Burnish with a burnishing brush or soft cloth to remove the excess leaf and continue gilding until the whole area is covered.

**5** Paint a thin, even coat of water-based varnishing wax on to the gilded surface. Leave to dry for 2–3 hours, then buff with a soft cloth.

**6** Using a fine brush, dab some spots of amber French enamel varnish on to the gilded surface to create the illusion of rust. Leave to dry for 30 minutes.

**7** Mix some black acrylic paint with a little water. Paint random areas of the bottom part of the pot black, keeping the strokes diagonal. Leave to dry for 1 hour.

**8** Mix some ultramarine acrylic paint with a little white and some water. Paint some more random areas of the bottom part of the pot in this colour. Leave to dry for 1 hour.

**9** Mix three acrylic colours with water in separate paint pans: yellow-ochre, white and black. Load an old stiff-bristled brush with one colour at a time and flick the bristles back to give a fine spray of dots over the surface of the pot.

**10** Make a verdigris colour by mixing two parts viridian-green acrylic paint with one part white and a little water. Fill the flower mister with water and test the spray.

**11** Place the amphora on an old sheet or towel. Paint some verdigris colour on to the top half of the amphora and disperse with the flower mister so that the colour dribbles down the pot. Continue until you have the desired verdigris effect. Leave to dry for 2–3 hours.

**12** Paint the whole pot with a thin, even coat of water-based matt (flat) varnish. Leave to dry for 2–3 hours.

# Hat Box

*Plain cardboard gift boxes can be bought in all shapes and sizes from most craft shops, stationers and department stores. Sumptuous velvet and gilded cherubs transform this simple box into a beautiful gift for a loved one that will be treasured for years. The box can be used to store many treasures and precious items – not just hats*

**YOU WILL NEED**

plain cardboard gift box
ruler or measuring tape
paper, for pattern
pencil
red velvet
tailor's chalk
scissors
gold taffeta or lining material
PVA (white) or fabric glue
5mm/¹/₄ in paintbrush
pins
gold-coloured sewing
   thread
needle
florist's wire
dried flowers and pods
cherub decoration
gold spray paint
bradawl
wire cutters

1 Measure the box lid and sides and make paper templates the same size. Transfer on to the velvet using tailor's chalk. Cut around the template, leaving a 2.5cm/1in seam allowance all the way around. Cut small slits to the chalk line.

2 Lay the box and lid on the taffeta or lining material and draw two ovals approximately 25cm/10in larger all round. Stick the first velvet piece to the base of the box using PVA (white) or fabric glue, sticking the cut slits on to the sides of the box.

3 Next, stick the velvet side piece to the box, painting on the glue and folding over the cut slits to make a neat edge. At the top edge, fold and stick the velvet on to the inside of the box. Repeat with the lid.

4 Gather the lining piece into the base of the box and pin in place. Using small stitches and gold-coloured thread, oversew the lining around the inside edges to hide the rough velvet edges. Repeat with the lining for the lid.

5 Wire the dried flowers and pods together with the cherub in a pleasing arrangement. Spray with gold paint, making sure that the whole area is covered, and leave to dry for 30 minutes.

6 Make two holes in the box with a bradawl. Thread some florist's wire through to the inside of the box, loop over the arrangement and thread through the second hole. Wind the ends of the wire together neatly and trim with wire cutters.

# CONTEMPORARY TRAY

*This plain wooden tray has been totally transformed into a stylish accessory for a modern home. The contemporary appearance is created by the use of aluminium leaf and bronze powders and is bound to attract admiring comments. When varnished, the tray will stand up to normal wear and tear*

**YOU WILL NEED**

plain wooden tray
dark blue spray paint
water-based size
2.5cm/1in paintbrush
aluminium leaf
burnishing brush or soft cloth
pencil
stencil cardboard
craft knife
cutting mat
stencil brush
face mask
copper powder
saucer
5cm/2in paintbrush
acrylic satin varnish

1 Spray the tray with two coats of dark blue spray paint, leaving to dry for 1 hour between coats. Paint a thin, even coat of water-based size on to the top rim of the tray.

2 Leave the tray to dry for 20–30 minutes, until the size becomes clear and tacky. Gild with aluminium leaf and burnish with a burnishing brush or soft cloth to remove excess leaf.

3 Trace the templates from the back of the book and transfer to the stencil cardboard. Using a craft knife and cutting mat, cut out the stencils.

4 Position the stencils on the base of the tray. Using a stencil brush, stipple water-based size through the stencils. Remove the stencils. Leave for 20–30 minutes, until the size becomes clear and tacky.

5 Wearing a mask, tip some copper powder on to a saucer. Pick up some powder with a 5cm/2 in brush and brush over the sized areas. Remove the excess powder with a burnishing brush or soft cloth.

6 Seal the tray with two to three coats of acrylic satin varnish, leaving 2–3 hours between coats.

# ICON PAINTING

*It might seem rather a daunting project to make your own icon, but with care (and a little cheating), you can reproduce a beautiful medieval-style painting. Gilding is used to add antique authenticity and the deep red tones of the painting match those of Italian religious frescoes. This technique can be used for the image of your choice*

**YOU WILL NEED**

small piece of plain wood or MDF (medium density fibreboard)
chisel
sandpaper
acrylic wood primer
2.5cm/1in paintbrush
reference for icon picture
tracing paper
pencil
assorted acrylic paints
paint pan
red acrylic gesso
assorted acrylic bristle brushes
artist's palette
water-based size
gold Dutch metal leaf
burnishing brush or soft cloth
wire (steel) wool
methylated spirit (methyl alcohol)
amber shellac varnish
amber French enamel varnish
chalkboard paint
quick-drying clear matt (flat) acrylic varnish

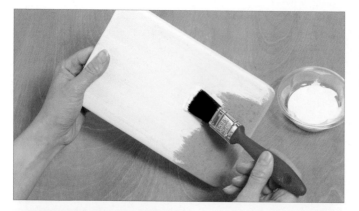

**1** Use a chisel to roughen the edges of the wood or MDF (medium density fibreboard) and sand down. Prime with acrylic primer and leave to dry for 1–2 hours.

**2** Trace or copy the basic icon design from a reference book or other source, or devise your own design.

3 Transfer the tracing to the wood and fill in the details of the design freehand with a pencil.

4 Dilute some acrylic paint for the background with a little water, and apply with an acrylic bristle brush.

5 Leave the background to dry. Paint the halo and sleeve band in red acrylic gesso and leave to dry for 30–40 minutes.

6 Finish the painting, keeping the colours pale and as close to those of the original as possible to give the illusion of age. Leave to dry thoroughly.

7 Paint a thin, even coat of water-based size on to the halo and sleeve band and leave for 20–30 minutes, until the size becomes clear and tacky.              ➤

**8** Gild the halo and sleeve band using gold Dutch metal leaf. Burnish with a burnishing brush or soft cloth to remove the excess leaf and to add lustre. Dip some wire (steel) wool into a little methylated spirit (methyl alcohol). Rub the gilding to reveal some of the base coat.

**9** Paint a thin, even coat of amber shellac on to the gilded areas and leave to dry for 30 minutes to 1 hour. Using French enamel varnish, paint the halo and sleeve band. Leave to dry for 30 minutes. Use chalkboard paint to add details.

**10** When completely dry, lightly sand the rest of the painting to distress it. Do not rub too hard.

**11** Paint the edges of the wooden block in chalkboard paint and leave to dry for 3–4 hours.

**12** Seal the entire painting and the sides with quick-drying matt (flat) acrylic varnish and leave to dry for 3–4 hours.

# ℕ APKIN RINGS

*These napkin rings will add a touch of theatrical*

*glamour to your dining table. They started life as*

*plastic piping and were embellished cheaply using*

*Dutch metal leaf and plastic jewels to create*

*deceptively expensive-looking accessories from*

*virtually nothing. Look out for interesting beads and*

*other decorative items for further embellishments.*

*Bead shops and haberdashers are often a good source.*

*These rings look fabulous with snow-white linen*

*napkins for a really classy look* ◌

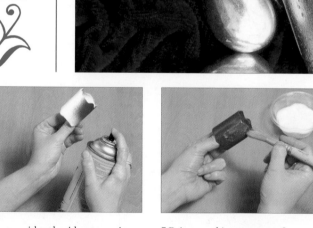

**YOU WILL NEED**

plastic piping
black felt-tipped pen
coping saw
sandpaper
red oxide spray primer
water-based size
2.5cm/1in paintbrushes
Dutch metal leaf in gold and
  aluminium

burnishing brush or soft
  cloth
amber shellac varnish
dome-shaped jewels
glue gun and glue sticks

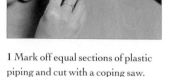

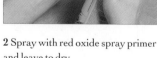

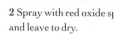

1 Mark off equal sections of plastic piping and cut with a coping saw. Sand down the edges until smooth.

2 Spray with red oxide spray primer and leave to dry.

3 Paint on a thin, even coat of water-based size and leave for 20–30 minutes, until it becomes clear and tacky.

4 Carefully lay the gold Dutch metal leaf on to the surface to cover the whole area. Use a burnishing brush or soft cloth to remove the excess leaf and bring up the lustre.

5 Seal with a thin, even coat of amber shellac varnish and leave to dry for 45 minutes to 1 hour.

6 Glue dome-shaped jewels around the centre of the napkin rings using a glue gun.

# CHERUB BOX

*As the trend for paint effects gains momentum, unpainted medium density fibreboard, or MDF, items are becoming more easily available and can be found in many outlets. This simple hinge-lidded box has a classic look, which is enhanced by gilding, and given a baroque appearance by adding a cherub*

**YOU WILL NEED**

small wooden box with hinge
glue gun and glue sticks
cherub Christmas decoration
red oxide paint
2.5cm/1in paintbrushes
water-based size
gold Dutch metal leaf
burnishing brush or soft cloth
wire (steel) wool
methylated spirit (methyl
alcohol)
amber shellac varnish
pink acrylic paint
paint pan
soft cloth

1 Use a glue gun to stick the cherub at an angle to the top of the box. Leave to dry for 10 minutes.

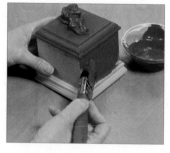

2 Prime the box with red oxide paint and leave to dry for 1–2 hours.

3 Paint on a thin, even coat of water-based size and leave for 20–30 minutes, until clear and tacky.

4 Gild the surface with gold Dutch metal leaf, ensuring that the whole area is covered. Burnish with a burnishing brush or soft cloth to remove the excess leaf and bring up the lustre.

5 Dip some wire (steel) wool into a little methylated spirit (methyl alcohol) and rub to reveal some of the base coat. Seal with a thin, even coat of amber shellac and leave to dry for 30 minutes to 1 hour.

6 Mix some pink acrylic paint with water and paint over the surface. Rub off most of the paint with a cloth, leaving only a little paint in the details. Leave to dry for 30 minutes.

# Medieval Clock

*This amazing medieval-style clock started life as a plastic wall clock that
was found broken and discarded. By adding medium density fibreboard
and using various simple techniques, including gilding of course, the
clock was given an astounding transformation to make it a stunning
addition to any interior*

### YOU WILL NEED

old school or office wall clock

sandpaper

1.8cm/³/₄ in thick, MDF (medium density
  fibreboard), 80cm/32in square

felt-tipped pen

jigsaw

pair of compasses (or string and pen)

general-purpose sealant and gun

cardboard

craft knife

wood glue

nails

hammer

artist's palette

petroleum jelly

filler

filling knife

2.5cm/1in paintbrushes

white acrylic primer

red emulsion (latex) paint

water-based size

Dutch metal leaf in aluminium, gold
  and copper

burnishing brush or soft cloth

amber shellac varnish

water-based varnishing wax

soft cloths

acrylic paints in purple and green

paint pan

2mm/¹/₁₆ in thick cardboard

drill

clock movement

red oxide spray primer

1 Dismantle the clock, removing and
discarding the old movement, hands
and glass. Wash the remaining parts
of the clock in hot soapy water. Sand
down the clockface and surround
with sandpaper and reassemble the
basic clock.

2 Trace the template from the back
of the book. Transfer on to the MDF
(medium density fibreboard) with
the felt-tipped pen, using the clock
surround as a guide for scaling up
the shape.

3 Using a jigsaw fitted with a narrow
blade, cut out the shape. Cut out a
circle in the centre slightly smaller
than the clock surround to allow
access to the back of the clock. Sand
down all the edges.

**4** Using a general-purpose sealant gun, glue the clock surround on to the MDF, applying thick beading to the outside edge and a larger amount of sealant to the inside edge at the back. Leave to dry for 24 hours.

**5** Make a cardboard template of the raised areas of the cross. Cut a piece of MDF to the same width as the template, then draw round the template four times on to the MDF. Cut out the pieces with the jigsaw and sand the edges.

**6** Using a craft knife, shave off the bottom of the edge of each piece where it will meet the line of sealant around the clock surround. Fix with wood glue and nail the pieces in position with a small hammer. ➤

**7** Grease a small artist's palette with petroleum jelly and fill four compartments with filler. Leave to dry, pop from the mould, and stick one in the centre of each raised piece.

**8** Mix the filler into a thick paste and use a filling knife to spread it over the entire clock. Try to maintain an even thickness of approximately 3mm/¹/₈ in all over.

**9** Dip a 2.5cm/1in paintbrush in water and smooth the surface with a stroking action in the same direction. Work your way around the clock 2–3 times. Leave to dry.

**10** Lightly sand the high parts and rough edges. Apply a coat of acrylic primer and leave to dry for 1–2 hours. Paint on a coat of red emulsion and leave for 2–3 hours.

**11** Apply water-based size to the areas you wish to gild in aluminium. Leave for 20–30 minutes. Gild with aluminium and burnish. Gild gold areas with gold Dutch metal leaf.

**12** Seal gold areas with two coats of amber shellac varnish and aluminium areas with water-based varnishing wax. Leave the wax to dry, then buff with a soft cloth.

13 Mix purple acrylic paint with a little water and apply all over. Leave to set for 5 minutes, then rub off most of the paint with a cloth, leaving a little paint in areas of detail.

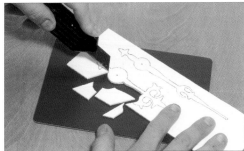

14 Trace the hands from the back of the book on to cardboard and cut out. Drill two holes slightly larger than the holes in the hands supplied with the clock movement.

15 Snip the supplied hands to fit the new hands and glue on to the back of the new hands. Spray the hands with red oxide spray primer and leave to dry for 1 hour.

16 Size the hands and leave for 20–30 minutes, until the size is clear and tacky. Gild with crumpled copper Dutch metal leaf.

17 Roughly dab some green acrylic paint on to the hands using random brush strokes. Using a damp cloth, dab on more paint to build up the crusty effect.

18 Following the manufacturer's instructions, fit the new movement to the clock face and fit the hands. Add a dab of paint to the fixing nut to finish.

# HARVEST POD BOX

*This lovely gilded box frame with its woodwashed interior is used to display an arrangement of gilded pods, roots and fruits in a celebration of autumnal bounty. The box is quite simple to make and you can have the glass cut to size at the store if you prefer not to do it yourself. This project shows how gilding can highlight the texture and shapes of natural objects beautifully*

**YOU WILL NEED**

length of pine, 6.5cm x 5mm/
  2¹/₂ x ¹/₄ in
ruler
pencil
saw
mitre saw
1.5cm/¹/₂ in panel pins (brads)
hammer
length of tongue and groove
  pine
azure-blue matt emulsion
  (flat latex) paint
paint pan
2.5cm/1 in bristle brushes

sandpaper
deep recess hockey stick
  framing
picture glass
glass-cutter (optional)
red oxide primer
water-based size
Dutch metal leaf in gold,
  copper and aluminium
burnishing brush or soft cloth
dried fruits and pods
amber shellac varnish
transparent acrylic varnish
white wax crayon
glue gun and glue sticks

1 Cut the pine to the required lengths to build the sides of the box. Use a mitre saw or make butt joints, whichever you prefer, and tack together with panel pins (brads). Cut the tongue and groove pine to the required size to make a base for the box.

2 Thin down the emulsion (latex) paint and paint the sides of the box and the lengths of tongue and groove blue. Leave to dry for 30 minutes. Lightly sand the painted pieces to create an aged effect. Tack the tongue and groove pine to the sides with panel pins.

3 To make the frame, measure and cut the hockey stick framing using a mitre saw, so that it easily slides over the sides of the box.

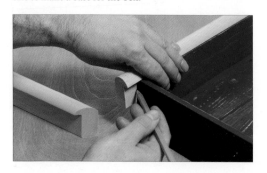

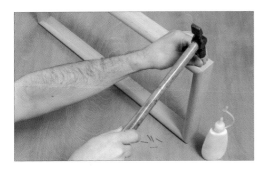

4 Tack the frame together with panel pins (brads).

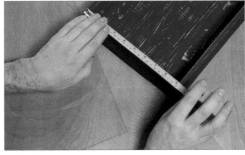

5 Measure and cut the glass to fit inside the frame.

6 Paint the frame with red oxide primer and leave to dry for 2–3 hours. Paint on a thin, even coat of water-based size and leave for 20–30 minutes, until it becomes clear and tacky. Gild with gold Dutch metal leaf, crushing the leaf as you go along to create a broken effect. Burnish with a burnishing brush or soft cloth to remove the excess leaf.

7 Paint the fruits and pods with red oxide primer and leave to dry. Paint on water-based size and leave for 20–30 minutes, until it becomes clear and tacky. Gild some of the pods and fruits with copper Dutch metal leaf, some with gold and some with aluminium, crushing the leaf as before. Burnish with a burnishing brush or soft cloth.

8 Seal the gold frame, pods and fruits with amber shellac varnish and leave to dry for 45 minutes to 1 hour.

9 Seal the aluminium and copper pods and fruits with transparent acrylic varnish and leave to dry for 1–2 hours.

**10** Arrange the pods and fruits in rows on the base of the box and mark their positions with a white wax crayon. Use the glue gun to glue them in place and leave to dry.

**11** Fit the glass over the pods and slide the frame into place.

**12** Secure the frame to the box with panel pins (brads).

# HEART BROOCH AND HAT PIN

*This little brooch is made from medium density fibreboard and gilded using a distressed technique. The delicate heart-shaped pin is made from modelling clay, and is gilded and decorated with jewels*

### YOU WILL NEED

piece of MDF (medium density fibreboard), 10cm / 4in square

black felt-tipped pen

coping saw

sandpaper

pale blue spray paint

water-based size

two bristle brushes

gold Dutch metal leaf

burnishing brush or soft cloth

wire (steel) wool

methylated spirit (methyl alcohol)

acrylic varnishing wax

soft cloth

glue gun and glue sticks

brooch back

hat pin and cap

modelling clay

rolling pin

modelling tools

gilt cream

soft cloth

plastic jewels

## HEART BROOCH

1 Draw a heart shape on the MDF (medium density fibreboard) with a black felt-tipped pen. Cut the shape out with a coping saw. Roughen the edges with sandpaper to add texture.

2 Spray both sides of the heart with pale blue spray paint and leave to dry. Paint a thin, even coat of water-based size on to the front of the heart and leave for 20–30 minutes, until it becomes clear and tacky.

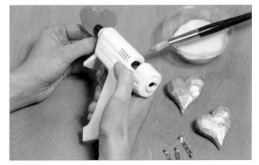

3 Cover the sized area with gold Dutch metal leaf. Remove the excess with a burnishing brush or soft cloth. Distress the surface using wire (steel) wool and a little methylated spirit (methyl alcohol).

4 Seal with acrylic varnishing wax and leave to dry. Buff with a soft cloth. Glue a brooch back on to the back of the heart. ➤

## HEART HAT PIN

**1** Warm and roll out the modelling clay to a thickness of about 5mm/¹⁄₄ in. Cut out a heart and round off the edges. Use modelling tools to make patterns and indentations in the clay.

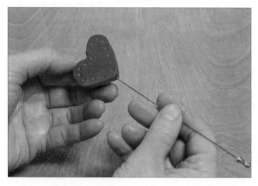

**2** Insert the hat pin into the base of the heart to a depth of about 2.5cm/1in. Enlarge the hole slightly by circling the pin, then remove the pin. Bake the heart in the oven following the manufacturer's instructions. Leave to cool.

**3** Rub gilt cream into both sides of the heart and leave to dry. Buff with a soft cloth.

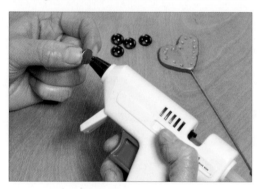

**4** Glue the hat pin into the base of the heart and glue plastic jewels on to the heart.

*Left: Make a series of hat pins to give as gifts.*

# STAR COOKIES AND COASTERS

*Stars have always been a source of wonder and fascination. There are many different star shapes, so experiment with your own designs. Gilded stars make beautiful ornaments and, although they are mostly associated with Christmas, there is no reason why stars shouldn't decorate your home at any time of the year* ∽

**YOU WILL NEED**

scissors
24-carat edible gold leaf
thin cardboard
fine paintbrush
piping jelly (gel)
cookies, bought or home-made
stencil brush
squares of MDF (medium density fibreboard)
black felt-tipped pen
coping saw
sandpaper
dark blue spray paint
water-based size
2.5cm/1in paintbrushes
gold Dutch metal leaf
burnishing brush or soft cloth
wire (steel) wool
methylated spirit (methyl alcohol)
amber shellac varnish
sticky-backed felt

## STAR COOKIES

1 Cut out star shapes from the edible leaf. Avoid handling it too much as it will spoil the shine.

2 Make a star stencil from thin cardboard. Use a fine paintbrush to paint piping jelly (gel) through the shape on to each cookie.

3 Lay the gold stars paper side up on to the piping jelly using the stencil as a guide. Press down firmly with a stencil brush and peel away the backing paper. Leave to harden for 24 hours. ➤

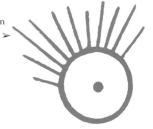

## STAR COASTERS

1 Draw the star shape on the medium density fibreboard and cut out with a coping saw. Round off the edges with sandpaper.

2 Prime the star on both sides with dark blue spray paint and leave to dry. Paint a coat of water-based size on both sides and leave for 20–30 minutes, until clear and tacky.

3 Gild both sides of the star with gold Dutch metal leaf. Burnish with a burnishing brush or soft cloth to remove the excess leaf. Dip some wire (steel) wool into a little methylated spirit (methyl alcohol) and gently distress the edges of the star.

4 Seal on both sides with a thin, even coat of amber shellac varnish and leave to dry for 45 minutes to an hour. Cut out a star from sticky-backed felt, peel off the backing paper and carefully stick to one side of the star.

*Left: The finished coasters can be used as a base for candles.*

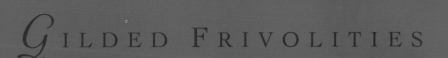

# GILDED FRIVOLITIES

Let your imagination run wild, and consider gilding all kinds of items, from fir cones and pebbles, to your very own gilded birdcage! Any item, no matter how unassuming, will benefit from a touch of gold.

# GILDING THE LILY

N ow that you are familiar with the techniques and possibilities of gilding, the fun really starts. Gilding is the ultimate way to make your mark on all manner of objects for the home all year round. Gilding food is the last word in decadence, and has been practised by the Indian nobility for centuries – astound your dinner guests by indulging in the Midas touch. Traditionalists might shudder at the idea of gilding nuts and shells, but, like many natural materials, the textures provide a wonderful surface to work on, and with the array of reasonably priced composite leaf on offer, projects such as these are not as costly as it might appear. Old pieces of

*Above: This astrological clockface is enhanced with gold Dutch metal leaf.*

driftwood are also worth salvaging from the beach; their wonderful gnarled appearance further embellished with composite leaf, to create a striking contemporary piece.

Gilded items make exquisite gifts that will be treasured by the recipient, transforming the mundane into something truly spectacular. You needn't restrict yourself to gold tones, either; composite leaf exists in almost any metallic shade, so let your imagination run riot, and look out for interesting shapes and textures to create unique objects that are every bit as beautiful as more traditional pieces.

*Left: Decorative plaster shells are embellished with gold and silver leaf.*

*Right: Silver metallic powder was used sparingly, but to great effect, on this polymer clay frame.*

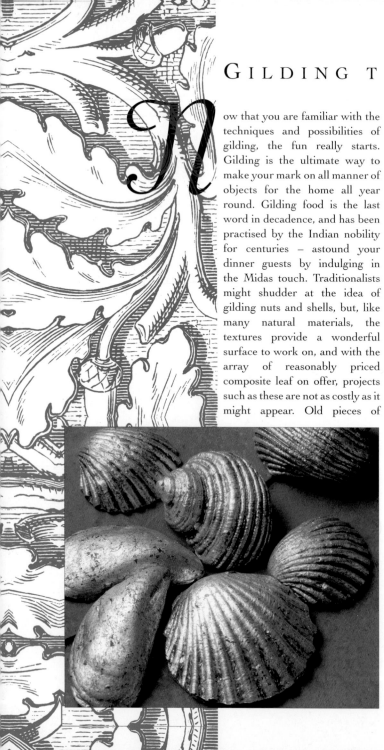

# GILDED BIRDCAGE

*Now you can have your own bird in a gilded cage!*
*This pretty, old-fashioned birdcage was found in a*
*junk shop. A rusted gilt technique is used here, as it*
*is an easier way of gilding awkwardly shaped*
*objects. Filling the many nooks and crannies with*
*broken leaf ensures that as much of the cage as*
*possible is covered* ☾

**YOU WILL NEED**

birdcage
red oxide spray primer
water-based size
2.5cm/1in paintbrushes
old sheet (optional)
broken gold Dutch metal leaf
  (schlag)
dish
soft-bristled brush
water-based clear matt (flat)

varnish
powder pigment in burnt
  umber and yellow-ochre
paint pans
soft cloth (optional)

1 Spray an even coat of red oxide
spray primer over the birdcage
inside and out. Using spray primer
makes covering the whole cage
much easier than using a paintbrush
and ensures an even coverage.

2 Paint water-based size on to the
cage, making sure the whole cage is
covered inside and out. Access the
interior through the cage door.
Leave the size for about 20–30
minutes, until it becomes tacky
and clear.    ➤

**3** Place the cage on a sheet to collect any of the broken leaf. Pour the leaf in a dish and sprinkle the leaf on to the cage.

**4** Re-size any patchy areas and use the excess leaf caught in the sheet or on the work surface to fill them in.

**5** Burnish the cage with a soft brush until all the loose leaf has been removed and the surface is as smooth as possible.

**6** Pour some water-based varnish into two saucers or paint pans and add burnt umber pigment to one and yellow-ochre pigment to the other.

**7** Using a separate brush for each colour, dab on patches of the two colours to build up a rust effect. Don't make the dabs too heavy and make sure that some of the leaf is still visible. Wipe gently with a cloth if necessary.

**8** Continue until the whole surface is covered and leave to dry for 1–2 hours. The varnish will seal the surface, so there is no need for further sealing.

# Star  tree  decorations

*These simple tree ornaments are easy to make*

*from medium density fibreboard using a coping*

*saw. Gilded using a distressed technique and*

*embellished with a single bead and ribbon, they*

*make long-lasting and individual decorations.*

*Hang them individually from a Christmas tree,*

*or in groups on lengths of different ribbons* ∽

**YOU WILL NEED**
15cm/6in squares of MDF
  (medium density fibreboard)
black felt-tipped pen
coping saw or fretsaw
sandpaper
electric or hand drill
red oxide spray primer
water-based size
2.5cm/ in bristle brushes
Dutch metal leaf in gold and
  aluminium

burnishing brush or soft cloth
wire (steel) wool
methylated spirit (methyl
  alcohol)
shellac varnish
acrylic varnishing wax
acrylic paints in green and blue
paint pans
soft cloths
glue gun and glue sticks
dome-shaped plastic jewels
lengths of ribbon

1 Trace the template from the back
of the book. Draw the star shape
on to the MDF (medium density
fibreboard) using a fine black felt-
tipped pen.

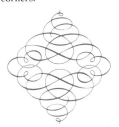

2 Using a coping saw or fretsaw,
carefully cut out the shape. Sand
down any rough edges and smooth
the corners.     ➤

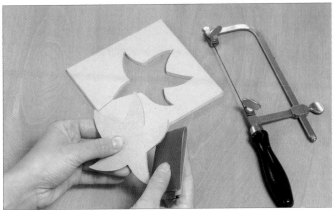

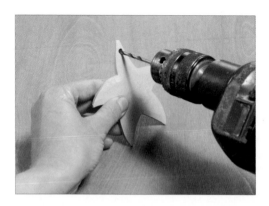

**3** Mark a dot just in from the end of one point. Drill a hole with an electric or hand drill.

**4** Spray both sides of the star with red oxide spray primer and leave to dry.

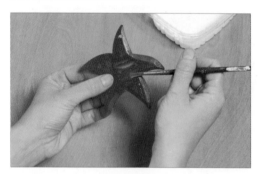

**5** Paint on a thin, even coat of water-based size and leave for 20–30 minutes, until it becomes clear and tacky. Gild some stars with gold and some with aluminium Dutch metal leaf.

**6** Burnish the stars with a burnishing brush or soft cloth. Dip some wire (steel) wool into a little methylated spirit (methyl alcohol) and distress the edges of each star. Paint an even coat of shellac on to the gold leaf and acrylic varnishing wax on to the aluminium leaf.

**7** In separate containers, mix some green and blue acrylic paint with a little water. Paint the gold stars green and the aluminium stars blue. Leave to set for 5 minutes, then remove most of the paint with a cloth. Dampen the cloth if the paint has set too much. Stick a dome-shaped jewel into the centre of each star and tie a ribbon through each hole for hanging.

# G ILDED   NUTS

*Nuts are ideal subjects for gilding as they have so
much texture and detail and they can be put to all
sorts of decorative uses. They would make a
sumptuous table decoration for a party or look lovely
attached to gift boxes or in a bowl at Christmas* ∞

**YOU WILL NEED**

assorted nuts
red oxide spray primer
water-based size
2.5cm/¹/₂in paintbrushes
gold Dutch metal leaf
burnishing brush or soft
   cloth
amber shellac varnish

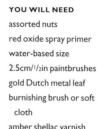

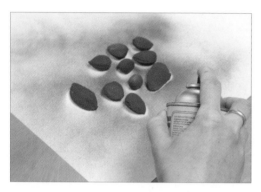

**1** Spray the nuts with red oxide spray primer and leave to dry for 30 minutes to 1 hour.

**2** Paint on a thin, even coat of water-based size and leave for 20–30 minutes, until it becomes clear and tacky.

**3** Wrap the sized nuts in sheets of gold Dutch metal leaf, making sure that they are completely covered and that no recesses or details are exposed.

**4** Burnish with a burnishing brush or soft cloth to remove the excess leaf. Seal with a thin, even coat of amber shellac varnish and leave to dry for 30 minutes to 1 hour.

# WOODEN BEAD NECKLACE

*Simple wooden balls available from craft stores are transformed by gilding to make a glittering necklace. Experiment with leaf or powders in different colours and alternate the colours of the beads on the string for stunningly original jewellery. This could also be used as a tie-back*

**YOU WILL NEED**

assorted wooden balls
vice
drill and fine bit
hammer
small nails
wood off-cut
red oxide spray primer
water-based size
2.5cm/1 in paintbrushes
Dutch metal leaf in gold,
copper and aluminium
burnishing brush or soft cloth
amber shellac varnish
acrylic varnishing wax
soft cloth
scissors
leather thongs

1 Holding each ball in turn in a vice, drill a hole through the centre.

2 Hammer small nails into the wood off-cut to make a rack. Place the balls on the nails and spray with red oxide primer. Leave to dry completely.

3 Paint a thin, even coat of water-based size on to the balls and leave for 20–30 minutes, until the size becomes clear and tacky.

4 Gild the balls in different colours of Dutch metal leaf and burnish with a burnishing brush or soft cloth to remove the excess leaf.

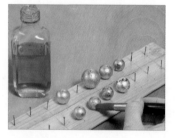

5 Seal the gold balls with amber shellac varnish and the copper and aluminium balls with acrylic varnishing wax. Buff up the wax with a soft cloth after 1–2 hours to bring up the lustre.

6 Cut lengths of leather thong and thread the balls on to it, alternating each colour. Tie the ends of the thong in a knot.

# GILDED STONES

*The texture and detail on stones make them ideal
candidates for gilding. They would make a pretty
edging for a path in a small garden or surprising
decorations for a rockery or border. As interior
decorations, they can be arranged in a conservatory
or garden room, or clustered around plant pots*

**YOU WILL NEED**

selection of stones and
  pebbles
white acrylic primer
2.5cm/1in paintbrush
water-based size
Dutch metal leaf in gold,
  aluminium and copper
burnishing brush or soft cloth
acrylic varnishing wax
soft cloth

1 Remove any earth or grit from the
stones, then wash them well and leave
to dry. Paint with white acrylic
primer and leave to dry for 1–2 hours.

2 Paint each stone with a thin coat
of water-based size and leave for
20–30 minutes, until it becomes clear
and tacky.

3 Lay the Dutch metal on to the
surface, one sheet at a time, to cover
the whole area, so that you have
several stones in each colour.
Burnish with a burnishing brush or
cloth to remove the excess leaf.

4 Seal each stone with a thin coat of
acrylic varnishing wax. Leave to dry
for 1–2 hours.

5 Buff up with a soft cloth to bring
up the lustre of the leaf.

# CHAPLET

*Dating back to Roman times, a chaplet is a wreath of leaves, gold and gems that was worn on the head on ceremonial occasions. This simple chaplet made from real laurel leaves is constructed using florist's wire and tape and is then sprayed gold for the imperial Roman touch*

**YOU WILL NEED**

laurel branch, with approximately 66 small, fresh leaves
florist's wire
wire cutters
florist's tape (stem wrap)
scissors
gold spray paint

**1** Gently pluck the leaves from the laurel, leaving a small stalk. If necessary, cut the florist's wire into 15cm/6in lengths.

**2** To single-leg mount the leaves, thread a wire through the leaf about 2.5cm/1in from the stalk. Twist the wire ends together to make a branch.

**3** Bind the stalks together with florist's tape (stem wrap), overlapping the leaves in pairs to make the two sides of the wreath.

**4** At the top end of each side of the wreath, make a hook in the wires. Hook the two sides together to make a circular shape, with the leaves pointing towards the front.

**5** Using florist's tape, attach more leaves at the base of the wreath to form a bow shape.

**6** Spray a fine mist of gold spray paint over the wreath, holding the can 30cm/12in away from the wreath and passing over several times to give an even coverage. Leave to dry for 30–40 minutes.

# FIR CONES

*The naturally intricate shape of fir (pine) cones looks wonderful when highlighted by the addition of gold spray and glitter. They could be arranged in a gilded bowl, to make a striking table decoration. They could also be arranged in a garland or wired individually and hung from a tree at Christmas time* ⌒

**YOU WILL NEED**

fir (pine) cones
red oxide spray primer
gold and silver sprays
glue gun and glue sticks
assorted glitters
saucer

1 To provide a good base colour for the gold spray, prime the cones with red oxide spray primer and leave to dry completely. Ensure all the recesses and details are well covered.

2 Spray the cones several times with gold or silver spray, so that you have several cones in different colours. Hold the can 25–30cm/10–12in away from the cones as you spray. Leave to dry.

3 Heat up the glue gun and apply a little glue to the tips of each cone. Be careful not to apply too much.

4 Working quickly, sprinkle the glitter on to the cones so that it sticks to the glued tips. Use a saucer to catch the excess glitter.

# DRIFTWOOD

*The twisted shapes of driftwood weathered by the elements make wonderful bases for gilding projects. Use the finished piece as an indoor or outdoor decoration at any time of year. Dutch metal transforms a naturally mysterious object into one of intriguing splendour*

**YOU WILL NEED**

driftwood
green spray paint
water-based size
5cm/2in paintbrushes
aluminium Dutch metal leaf
burnishing brush or soft cloth
water-based varnishing wax
soft cloth

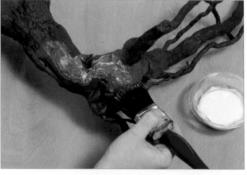

**1** Make sure that the wood is dry and remove any loose bits of wood or earth. Spray the entire surface with green spray paint and leave to dry for at least 1 hour.

**2** Paint on the water-based size, covering as much of the surface as possible. Leave for about 20–30 minutes, until the size becomes clear and tacky.

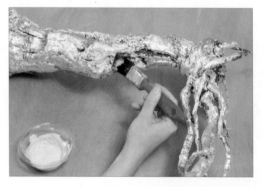

**3** Gild the wood with aluminium leaf and burnish with a burnishing brush or soft cloth to remove the excess leaf.

**4** Paint an even coat of varnishing wax over the surface. Leave to dry for 1 hour, then buff with a soft cloth.

# CHRISTMAS GARLAND

*Christmas is the obvious time of year for using gilding to decorate the home. The allure of shimmering metallic finishes adds to the magic of the season. This garland is made from dried flowers and other ornaments, sprayed gold and built up around a chicken wire tube. Collect a variety of objects, and experiment with different shapes and textures* ∞

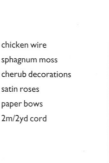

**YOU WILL NEED**

florist's wire
wire cutters
ruler
dried flowers, seedheads,
   pods, leaves and grasses
fresh ginger
pine cones
gold spray paint in three
   shades
chicken wire
sphagnum moss
cherub decorations
satin roses
paper bows
2m/2yd cord

**1** Cut the florist's wire into 20cm/8in lengths. Wrap the end of each natural item with a piece of wire, leaving 12cm/4½ in of wire protruding. Leaves and grasses may be bound together in bunches.

**2** Hold each piece by the end of the wire and spray with gold paint, so that you have several pieces in each of the three shades. Leave to dry for 30 minutes.

**3** Cut a piece of chicken wire 15cm/6in wide and as long as required. Curl up the edges and fill with moss. The moss will hold the gilded pieces, so make sure it is packed evenly.

4 Join the edges of the chicken wire together around the moss to make a tube. Pinch the edges of wire together to close the tube. Any stubborn gaps may be closed with florist's wire.

5 Push the wire ends of the gilded pieces through the chicken wire and into the moss, bending back the wire as you insert it for added security.

6 Continue to build up the garland, adding the cherub decorations, satin roses and paper bows to the gilded pieces to achieve the desired effect. Tie a length of cord to each end of the garland for hanging.

# GILDED INDIAN MEAL

*The Mogul Emperor Shahjehan who built the*
*beautiful Taj Mahal used to hold all-white banquets*
*within the Agra fort on nights with a full moon.*
*Everything was white and silver, including the food.*
*The leaf used here is perfectly edible*

**YOU WILL NEED**
scissors
edible silver leaf (warq)
tweezers

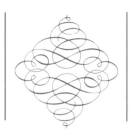

## WHITE CHICKEN KORMA
### (Safed Murgh Korma – Agra)

To serve four:

| | |
|---|---|
| 7.5ml/1½ tsp poppy seeds | clarified butter |
| 50g/2oz blanched almonds | 4 green cardamom pods |
| 50g/2oz unsalted cashew nuts | 2 cinnamon leaves or bay leaves |
| 3 chopped green chillies | 1 clove |
| 10ml/2 tsp chopped garlic | 1kg/2¼ lb boneless chicken breast portions |
| 10ml/2 tsp ground ginger | 2.5ml/½ tsp ground nutmeg |
| 350g/12oz chopped onions | 2.5ml/½ tsp ground mace |
| 45ml/3 tbsp ghee or | 300ml/½ pint/1¼ cups double (heavy) cream |

Heat a frying pan without any liquid and dry-roast the first seven ingredients. Cool, then grind to a fine paste.

Heat the ghee or clarified butter in a frying pan. Fry the cardamom, cinnamon and clove until the clove swells. Add the chicken and heat until it has released all its juices and is almost dry. Add the nutmeg, mace and prepared paste. Stir in the cream.

1 Place the chicken korma on to individual serving plates. Cut moon shapes from the edible leaf, carefully avoiding too much contact with the leaf, as this will dull the effect.

2 Using tweezers, gently place several moon shapes on top of the chicken korma. Serve with rice, garnishes and other accompaniments of your choice.

# $\mathcal{T}$EMPLATES

To enlarge templates to the size required, you can either use a photocopier, or a grid system.

For the grid system, trace the template from the book on to tracing paper, and draw a grid of evenly spaced squares over your tracing. To scale up, draw a larger grid on to another piece of paper. Copy the outline on to the second grid by taking each square individually and drawing the relevant part of the outline in the larger square. Finally, draw over the lines to make sure they are continuous.

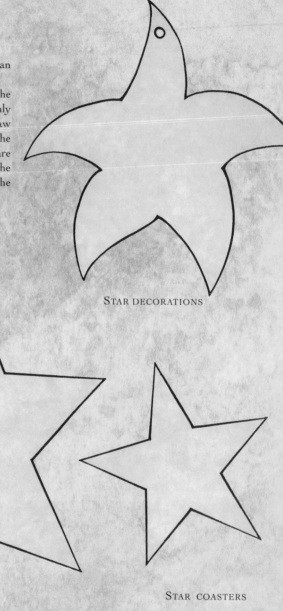

STAR DECORATIONS

STAR COASTERS

HEART CUSHION

STAR CUSHION

TILES

LAMPSHADE

VASE

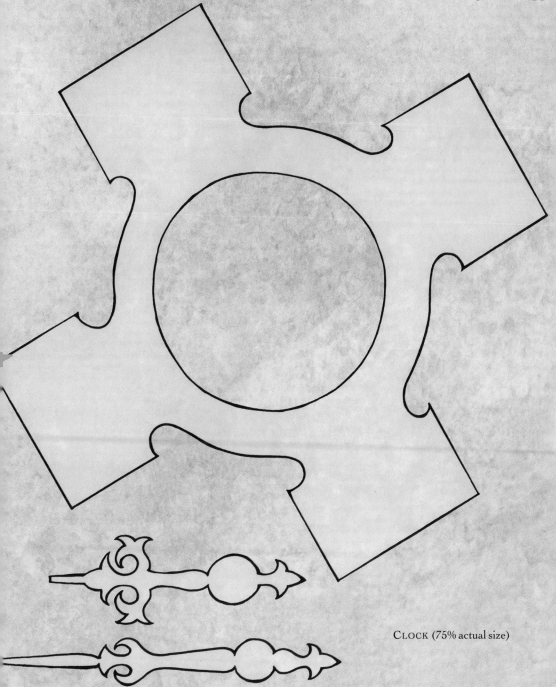

CLOCK (75% actual size)

# $S$ UPPLIERS

## UK

**Russell & Chapple**
68 Drury Lane
London WC2B 5SP
(020) 7836 7521
www.russellandchapple.co.uk
*Brushes, lacquer, metallic powders, oil
and acrylic paints and powder
pigments. Mail order.*

**L Cornelissen & Son Ltd**
105 Great Russell Street
London WC1B 3RY
(020) 7636 1045
www.cornelissen.com
*Gilding materials, powder pigments,
oil and acrylic colours. Mail order.*

**E. Ploton (Sundries) Ltd**
273 Archway Road
London N6 5AA
(020) 8348 0315
*Gold leaf and gilding supplies.
Mail order.*

**Green & Stone of Chelsea**
259 Kings Road
London SW3 5EL
(020) 7352 0837
www.greenandstone.com
sales@greenandstone.com
*Brushes, crackle varnish, linseed oil,
scumble glazes, shellac, stencil card
and other art materials and framing.*

**John Myland Ltd**
80 Norwood Road
West Norwood
London SE27 9NW
(020) 8670 9161
www.mylands.co.uk
*Gesso, polish, sandpaper and
wood finishes.*

**Plaster Works**
38 Cross Street
London N1 2BG
(020) 7226 5355
*Architectural cornices, mouldings and
other plaster objects and restoration.*

**Stuart Stevenson**
68 Clerkenwell Road
London EC1M 5QA
(020) 7253 1693
www.stuartstevenson.co.uk
*Gold and silver leaf and other gilding
and art materials. Mail order.*

**Minerva Art Supplies**
12A Trim Street
Bath BA1 1HB
(01225) 464054
www.minervaartsupplies.co.uk
*Brushes, lacquer, metallic powders, oil
and acrylic paints, gilding leaf and
powder pigments.*

**Scumble Goosi**
Unit 6b
Griffin Mill
London Road
Stroud
Gloucestershire GL5 2AZ
(01453) 731305
*Unpainted and painted MDF and
wooden interior accessories.
Mail order.*

## Sugar Celebrations
176a Manchester Road
Swindon SN1 1TU
(01793) 513549
www.sugar-celebrations.co.uk
*Edible gold leaf and piping gel.*
*Mail order.*

## CANADA

### Abbey Arts & Crafts
4118 Hastings Street
Burnaby, B.C.
(604) 299 5201
*Gilding and painting supplies.*

### Dundee Hobby Craft
1518-6551 No 3 Road
Richmond, B.C.
(604) 278 5713
*Gilding and painting supplies.*

### Michaels (Arts and Crafts Superstore)
200 North Service Road
Oakville Town Centre 2
Oakville, Ontario
(905) 842 1555
www.michaels.com
*Gilding and painting supplies.*

## USA

### Architectural Sculpture and Restoration
242 Lafeyette Street
New York, NY 10012
(212) 431 5873
www.asrnyc.com
*Ornamental plaster.*

### Art Essentials of New York
PO Box 38,
Tallman, NY 10982-0038

(845) 368-1100
www.artessentialsofnewyork.com
*Gilding supplies.*

### Creative Craft House
PO Box 2567
Bullhead City, AZ 86430
(520) 754 3300
*General craft supplies.*

### Blick Art Materials
PO.Box 1267
Galesburg, IL 61402-1267
www.dickblick.com
Order by phone: 1-800-828-4548
*All types of art supplies.*

### Esoteric Sign Supply
1644 Wilmington Boulevard
Wilmington,
California 90744
(310) 549 6622
www.esotericsignsupply.com
*Gilding supplies.*

### Frog Tool Company, Ltd.
2169 Illinois Route 26
Dixon, IL 61021
(815) 288 3811, (800) 648 1220
www.frogwoodtools.com
*Hand woodworking tools and finishing materials.*

### The Gold Leaf Company, Inc.
27 Fort Place - 2nd Floor
Staten Island NY 10301
(718) 815-8802
www.goldleafcompany.com
*Gilding supplies. Mail order only.*

### Klockit
PO Box 636
N3211 County Road H
Lake Geneva, WI 53147
1-800-556-2548
www.klockit.com
*Clock parts.*

### Sculpture House Casting
155 West 26th Street NY 10001
www.sculpturehousecasting.com
*Ornamental plaster.*

# $\mathcal{I}$ N D E X

## BIBLIOGRAPHY
*The Gilder's Manual*, The Society of Gilders, Excelsior Publishing House, New York.

*Practical Gilding*, by Peter and Anne McTaggart, Mac & Me Ltd, 1984.

*Sign Work: A Craftsman's Manual*, by Bill Stewart, Collins BSP, London, 1984.

*Formulas for Artists*, by Robert Massey, Batsford, London, 1968.

*The Craftsman's Handbook*, by Andrea Cennini, New York, 1960.

*The Romantic Interior: The British Collector at Home 1750–1850*, by Clive Wainwright, Yale University Press, 1989.

*Recipes for Surfaces*, by Mindy Drucker and Pierre Finkelstein, Cassell, London, 1993.

*Country Living Book of Paint Recipes*, by Liz Wagstaff, Quadrille, London, 1995.

## PICTURE CREDITS
The author and publishers would like to thank the following for the use of pictures reproduced in this book:
Bridgeman Art Library/Smithsonian Institution, Washington: p39 bottom; Bridgeman Art Library/Giraudon: p39 top; Lilli Curtiss: p12 bottom left and top, p13 bottom right; John Freeman: p10 bottom left and bottom right, p11, p38 top and bottom.

## AUTHOR'S ACKNOWLEDGEMENTS
My love and thanks to Mark for all his help and patience and to Netty for all her hard work, to Doug and Paul for their lovely pieces and to Clive and Jenny for the fun we had with the Chaplet, to Lucy and Debbie for their wonderful work and a big thanks to my editors Lindsay and Joanna for their understanding and support, and to all at Anness and the many others who cannot be mentioned here.